GOALS ACTION COURAGE VALUE INVEST GIVING LEGACY

7 CHECKLIST ITEMS FOR SUCCESS

A GUIDE TO A RICHER AND MORE SUCCESSFUL LIFE

JEAN G MATHURIN, M.D.

The views presented are those of the author
and do not necessarily represent the views of the
United States Department of Defense or the United States Navy.

ISBN: 978-1-7322884-6-1 (hardcover)
ISBN: 978-1-7322884-0-9 (paperback)
ISBN: 978-1-7322884-1-6 (epub)

Publisher's Cataloging-in-Publication Data
provided by Five Rainbows Cataloging Services

Names: Mathurin, Jean G., author.
Title: 7 checklist items for success : a guide to a richer and more successful life / Jean G. Mathurin, M.D.
Description: Pensacola, FL : 7 Checklist Items, 2018.
Identifiers: LCCN 2018905089 | ISBN 978-1-7322884-6-1 (hbk.) | ISBN 978-1-7322884-1-6 (ebook) | ISBN 978-1-7322884-2-3 (audiobook)
Subjects: LCSH: Success--Psychological aspects. | Wealth--Psychological aspects. | Motivation (Psychology) | Self-realization. | Inspiration. | Self-help techniques. | BISAC: SELF-HELP / Personal Growth / Success. | BODY, MIND & SPIRIT / Inspiration & Personal Growth.
Classification: LCC BF637.S8 M38 2018 (print) | LCC BF637.S8 (ebook) | DDC 650.1--dc23.

Printed in the United States.

This book is dedicated to my father,
Jean Lenord Mathurin.
His love for his children was unsurpassable.
I loved him, and I miss him every day.

This book is also dedicated to my nephew,
Walner Nelson, and all the young people of this world.
I hope this book will teach you the life lessons
I wish I had learned when I was your age.
May you have a life full of success and joy.

CONTENTS

PREFACE

Thank you for picking up this book. What you will undoubtedly notice is that the 7 *Checklist Items for Success* is not a book for everyone. It is not a book for the timid or for those who consider themselves passengers enjoying the ride of life, with no significant purpose and no desire to leave this world a little better than they found it. This book was written for those of you who know and believe at your core that you were created for something bigger than your current situation or circumstance in life. This book is for those who ask *why,* and want to find a way to make something happen. You crave a way to realize your full potential. The *why* of your existence is your core belief about *why* you are here on this earth. If you believe you are such a person, then this book is for you. As you read, you'll soon find this book will show you the *how* of these whys.

I wrote this book because I wish I had found such a book when I was fifteen. It took years for me to establish a cogent list that can help anyone, from any walk of life, achieve greater success in life.

You might be in a rough spot, wondering how you can possibly make it out. You might also be wondering: "How can this book help me succeed?" "Will this be a waste of my time?" "Is this book even worth the money I paid for it?" While my intention is not to answer these questions for you, I do believe you will find this book extremely valuable by the time you finish reading it.

Let me begin by sharing something that got my attention during my first year of residency in aerospace medicine in the United States

Navy. I was introduced multiple times to a graph that many in the aviation industry are quite familiar with: The graph shows the decrease of the Naval Aviation Mishap Rate from the 1950s to present. During their first year of training, many aerospace residents would often mutter under their breath that they hoped the professors would stop showing the graph because they believed the point had been made.

They thought they got it. Naval Aviation Mishap Rate has decreased a whole lot. Yet what this graph showed me went beyond how mishaps (aircraft accidents leading to fatalities) have decreased over time in the Navy. I intuitively understood that we were shown this graph again and again so that we understood that the decrease owes to the culture of safety in Naval Aviation.

While I was taking my introductory courses in Aviation, I was also introduced to something that I believed may have made the biggest contribution in reducing aircraft mishaps: a checklist in aviation. Going through the checklist items is a crucial aspect of what the pilot does from preflight to turning off the aircraft engine. This concept has been so successful in Aviation that it has also been used in the operating room.

The big question I asked myself was: If this checklist has proven to be so valuable in Aviation and now the surgical operating room, why not apply this same concept to people's lives to help them achieve their highest potential?

As a kid who grew up in poverty in Haiti, nothing would have been more beneficial to me than to pick up a textbook with some pointers that—if followed carefully, step-by-step—could bring me any success I could desire. When I started to research and ask around if such a checklist existed, one that when and if applied helped anyone to be successful in life, the answer was no. I set out to create one, so started reading all of the textbooks I could find on the subject of personal achievement. I also started to talk with some of the smartest people I know in different fields of study involving the mind (psychiatry, psychology) and those who have achieved the highest success in their various fields. Most of them told me that it would be hard to write a single book that would appeal to everyone. Many others have simply said that such an endeavor would be impossible because even though most people do want to be successful, everyone responds to different stimuli at a different time of their life. The likelihood that anyone would follow through with a checklist on a daily basis for many years seemed low. Thus, I was told that such a project would not be successful. These statements of impossibility resonated with me because, since I was a child, I had heard these words spoken to me many, many times.

In second grade, for example, my teacher told me that I was from a dumb family and that I would not amount to anything. Later, when I told some friends I wanted to become a physician, they said it was not possible. I was fortunate that my family believed in me, and with their support I have overcome many challenges. Perhaps it is because my desire for a more successful life was rooted so deeply that mere words of discouragement were not enough to derail me. Maybe my childhood challenges have made me more resilient, or maybe my desire for success goes beyond satisfying just my curiosity. Maybe I'm just stubborn. After my second-grade teacher told me that I was from a dumb family and would not amount to anything, I made up my mind right then and there that I would be a physician—just to prove her wrong.

While I was a dishwasher working at a casino, two months after I emigrated to the United States from Haiti, one of my co-workers—after I told him that my goal was to become a physician—insisted that it was impossible for someone like me (with limited English and no money) to study medicine. He said it was impossible given my circumstances. During the eighteen months I worked at that casino, my co-worker never failed to make fun of my dream of becoming a physician. His favorite joke was that Jesus would come before I ever became a doctor. His pessimism further invigorated my desire to become a physician, and ten years later, I not only achieved my goal, but I also have the greatest privilege of being a medical officer in the United States Navy.

My blessings have gone beyond even my wildest dreams and all I think of, knowing now that everything is possible, is that I should have dreamed of even more. If someone had told me as a young child that I would be able to reach this level of success in a foreign land called America, I honestly would have thought they were lying.

What you choose to believe in life about yourself can either break you down or build you up. In my case, I chose to believe my family. My challenges in life were also a blessing in disguise. They inspired me to start reading self-help books at the age of 15. During that time, most of my friends were focusing on the latest trends in clothes and how to be popular. My focus was different. I was more focused on how to improve my circumstances and the circumstances of those around me.

Now that my life has improved beyond belief, I hope this book will help improve your life—and those of others around you. I believe all that I have accomplished has only been possible thanks to the physician who saved my mother's life. I believe to this day that he did not only save my mother's life, but also saved the lives of my mother's eight children. Credit for my success in life, and credit for any benefits that you or anyone else might gain from reading and applying the ideas in this book, should go to that unnamed compassionate physician, and this should be proof enough of the circle of goodness and the passion of giving back more than one has received. This is a circle that I choose to believe and participate in, and I hope that you will also join. Please don't forget to write me if this book has helped you, because your experience may help someone else.

As a kid, I used to think that whenever I treated a future patient, I would want to receive a live turkey as my remuneration (more to come about that story later). Luckily for you, I have lowered my standards to just a few lines on the companion website for 7 *Checklist Items for Success*. Please take advantage and log on once you finish this book; spare yourself the hassle of mailing a live turkey. On a more serious note, while the meaning of success may be different for different people, it is my hope this book will help everyone looking for a guide to follow in their quest to attain their highest, noblest ideals—and a more successful life.

Presented within this book are ideas that helped me transform my life from famine to abundance—and, more importantly, ideas that have helped me to be more successful in every aspect of life. These ideas will also help you transform your life and the lives of those around you. I have read as many books as I could find about self-help in the last 25 years and, despite all the blessings I have received in life, I believe the ideas from these books have played the biggest role in transforming my life from a shy, poor Haitian kid to a board-certified physician and Naval Medical Officer in the United States.

My achievements can be attributed to grit, resilience, and delayed gratification. A tiny part of the credit goes to the motivation I gained from those who ridiculed my dreams, but the majority of my success is from the encouragement I received from those around me who believed in me and constantly prayed for my success and well-being. In case you have not yet been as lucky as I have been, this book is for you. I can say I have, for many years, recognized this desire to help improve people's lives by helping them focus on the opportunities around them instead of focusing on their misfortune.

My aspirations for writing a book stem from my faith in the limitless potential power we have as humans. I truly believe, if given the opportunity, we will choose good over evil, hope over despair, and joy over sadness. As a teenager in Haiti, I recall reading a French copy of *See You at the Top* by Zig Ziglar, which I purchased in front of the cathedral in Port-au-Prince. Before I read this book, I never believed that a life of success was really possible for someone like me. As I encountered other people at the top of their respective careers during my journey to a more successful life, I realized that my story is not unique.

That I have succeeded, as have others in similar (or even more dire) circumstances, will, I hope, bring you hope, help propel you to the top, create more value in your life and in the lives of those around you. I understand the critics will likely say that humans are complicated beings and that what works for one person may not work for the next; achieving the end goals promised by the author (in this case, me) is at best utopian. Those critics are making the same mistake that my second-grade teacher made: underestimating the limitless power of the individual.

I know your *why* (or your purpose in life) is big and your potential is limitless. This book will show you the *how* to have a more successful life. Such a book would have helped me tremendously in the pursuit and the achievement of my highest goals in life! I hope by providing a concise list to follow that you will garner great success, quicker than I did, and with fewer mishaps.

ABOUT ME

Two of my first memories, for some reason, have helped motivate me in my journey thus far. The first memory was that of me throwing up when my older sister, Yvenithe, was holding me in her arms trying to force me to eat a piece of fried egg and boiled plantain. My sister told me that I was probably three years old when this incident occurred, and we were living in the countryside of Sarazin, Mirebalais.

My second memory was that of feeding banana peels to a turkey that had one leg tied to a small, thin rope on the side of our one-bedroom house. I remember getting excited in anticipation of when my mother would cook that turkey. I was very sad when I learned that we would not be cooking the turkey and that my mother was fattening it up to give to the surgeon who had volunteered his time to remove the mass in my mother's abdomen. My parents could not even afford the medical supplies (including the medications) needed for the surgery. My mother was in the hospital for about a month, and, at the time, her doctors believed she wouldn't survive. Yet thanks to the generosity of that doctor, she did.

While mother cannot precisely explain what her medical diagnosis was, she bears two surgical scars from the surgical intervention of that one-month hospitalization. One is a vertical abdominal scar for removal of a mass in her abdominal cavity and another scar to her right mid-axillary area, where she had another mass removed from her chest cavity.

During that time, my dad sold nearly all his farmlands and livestock to pay for the discounted medical expenses to save my mother's life. His philosophy was that he would sell everything if he had to, even down to the last shirt on his back, for her. My dad used to say he would prefer to die first before he would stop taking care of his family.

Sadly, my father died on the February 27, 2011, after he helped all but one of my siblings emigrate to the United States. He was a grateful man and easy to please. I wish I could have spent more time with him, and I miss him dearly.

7 CHECKLIST ITEMS FOR SUCCESS

A GUIDE TO A RICHER
AND MORE SUCCESSFUL LIFE

GOALS   ACTION   COURAGE   VALUE   INVEST   GIVING   LEGACY

✔ 1. GOALS

Have goals for your life, short-term (daily to yearly goals) and long-term goals (1-10 year goals). Most importantly, have daily goals. Always remember that even the most skilled pilot flying the most sophisticated aircraft in the world will not be able to fly to his or her final destination without a flight plan and a clear destination. Even the best shot in the world cannot hit a target without aiming. Yet many of us conduct the most expensive vessel ever created—our life—without any goals. To call this insanity may be an understatement.

✔ 2. TAKE ACTION

Pledge to take action on every intuition and idea you conceive in your mind about your goals during the day. Apply *The 5 Second Rule* by Mel Robbins to take instant action on every goal-related thought. Your sub-conscious mind is always working to bring ideas, opportunities, and people to your life to help with your goals. Act on these intuitions; they are the voice of your subconscious.

✔ 3. COURAGE

Have the courage to go the extra mile with everything that you do, each and every time. Never let yourself be outworked by anyone. Working hard is the greatest equalizer in life. Have the courage to remain enthusiastic and do everything with a smile on your face and a genuine desire to help and serve those around you. Have the courage to be flexible and to adapt when the situation demands it. Have the courage to maintain your integrity at all costs. It takes years to develop a reputation for integrity, but it all can be lost in an instant.

✔ 4. VALUE RESOURCES

Your time is your most valued possession, but it is usually wasted by the poor while cherished like a treasure by the rich. Always remember that human resources, starting with yourself, are the greatest resources in the industry. Be genuinely interested and enthusiastic about everyone you meet. Learn about them and be sure to remember the name of everyone you meet. Always value yourself and adopt the appearance and the gravitas of a Chief Executive Officer. Others will judge you by your actions, your appearance, your character, and your communication. Dress in a way that someone would identify you among your peers as the CEO. Remember to fake it until you make it.

✔ 5. INVESTMENT

The most efficient way to invest in yourself is through hard work. Always invest in yourself in terms of learning about your profession. Seek to create value in yourself and in everyone around you. Always consider hard work to be the deposit into your account of success. While criticisms may act as unauthorized withdrawals from your success account, they can be converted to assets if you learn from them. Don't be cheated by them; instead, accept them objectively and learn to use them toward your growth.

✔ 6. GIVING BACK

Don't wait until you make it before giving back. Your cup doesn't have to be spilling over before you can start sharing the drink of hope for a more successful future to a thirsty soul in the desert of life. Seek to know what people around you want in life and help them get it. While it can be an uphill battle to become successful, always remember that just like a father wants the life of his children to be better than his own, so is the desire of your Creator. While you are on your quest to a more successful life (and even after realizing your goals), seek to invest in people. The truth is most people want to be successful, but the key is also to want to help others to be successful. The problem is most of them don't know where to start and are sometimes focused too much on what they do not have (i.e., lack of experience, lack of money, physical limitations). Any successful person knows that in the quest for success it is not what you *don't* have that will hold you back, but instead what you *do* have (i.e., your life, your passion, and your desires) that will make you successful. It is counter intuitive to focus on what's lacking when what you want is to become successful. Whatever you focus on will persist, grow, and continue to be the center of your focus and attention.

✔ 7. YOUR LEGACY

May your legacy be one of giving back and making a difference in the lives of people around you. Moving forward, you can lay the path to your legacy by applying the acts of kindness you have received along the way to your current situation. Moving forward, seek to perform more acts of kindness to others and give more in terms of the time you spend with them, the smiles you bestow on them, and the words of encouragement you speak unto them. Each one of us on this Earth is too precious and too rare to leave this world without making a positive impact in the life of those around us and the lives of those who will come after us.

CHAPTER 1

GOALS

Have goals for your life, short-term (daily to yearly goals) and long-term goals (1-10-year goals). Most importantly, have daily goals. Always remember that even the most skilled pilot flying the most sophisticated aircraft in the world will not be able to fly to his or her final destination without a flight plan and a clear destination. Even the best shot in the world cannot hit a target without aiming. Yet many of us conduct the most expensive vessel ever created—our life—without any goals. To call this insanity may be an understatement.

STARTING IS HARD, BUT ESSENTIAL

You deserve to be congratulated for starting this book. At this point, you may not know what your goals are; you may not even be sure of how to develop your goals for a more successful life. This is completely okay. The important thing is that you have started, and you are reading this chapter.

I first started keeping specific goals for my life when I was 15. At that age, it was not easy for me to set long-term goals, so I defaulted to setting short-term goals that I could achieve within one year. Later, as I gained confidence in my ability to realize my goals, I started to set more long-term goals, which I planned to achieve within one to ten years.

When I was younger, my family and I lived in Haiti, where my options were limited. Some of the most intelligent upper classmen I knew were not able to afford to go to college, so setting goals to study in the United States at that time would have seemed impossible; instead, I set up goals to excel in each one of my classes. I was the seventh of eight children who had not finished high school. So, my goal became to finish high school. When I was in high school, I had no money to afford college, and I felt that I was on a dead-end road. But by that time, I was more confident in my ability to realize my goals, and even though it seemed impossible at that time, I set goals to go to college.

Your long-term goals may seem unrealistic based on your current situation, and that is okay because you want your goals to stretch you. What is not okay is to let yourself be discouraged by the naysayers or the people who don't even know you.

My neighborhood friends and my classmates considered me lucky because my dad lived in the U.S. They believed that all my needs were met, and unlike them, I never went to bed hungry at night. This was only partly true. Although my mother tried the best she could to give my siblings and I at least one meal per day, the truth was that it was never enough to feed eight hungry mouths.

Even worse, I truly had an insatiable appetite, more so than any of my other siblings. I used to say I needed more food because I burned more energy walking forty-five minutes to school. This justification was immediately refuted by my siblings, because they also had to walk the same distance. Later, I came up with a better excuse: I explained that my brain needed more energy to learn than theirs did. They could not argue with that because I had better grades than them—though the real reason they kept quiet was that they were sick and tired of listening to me whine and cry for food.

Sadly, not having enough to eat was a common theme among my neighborhood friends and classmates. Even today, I still have to face the fact that while I am successful, many people that I grew up with still live in poverty.

My dad, Jean Lenord Mathurin, was a forty-five-year-old illiterate Haitian farmer who, after selling almost everything he had to pay for his wife's medical bills, decided to sell everything else he owned to pay for a one-way boat fare to the U.S. in 1984. Of course, my dad did not know anyone in the U.S., and there was no way for him to guarantee that life would be any better there. I asked him, before he passed away in 2011, why he made such a desperate choice to move to the United States. My father told me how much he loved his children and wife and how devastated he was looking at us going hungry in front of him.

He told me that after my mother's hospitalization, the remaining farmlands he had could not produce enough food (usually plantain and yam) even to provide for his family. Moreover, some of what he grew had to be sold so my mother could buy salt to boil them and occasionally buy smoked herring for gravy.

I remember my father sharing his portion of food with my siblings and me. He stated the first time he saw me licking my plate to get every scrap of food, he knew he had to do something more. He had a goal to be able to feed his family comfortably and give us a better life. The only feasible choice he had was to risk his life to go to the U.S., where he found work as a farmhand and later in a packing house. Most of the time he started at five in the morning and worked until eleven at night to pay for his living expenses in the U.S. and to feed us in Haiti.

To say setting and maintaining goals was hard while living in those conditions is an understatement. Yet my dad's struggle gave me the impetus to write my goals; focusing on them gave me a way to escape my daily difficulties.

Looking back, I think having goals was even therapeutic for me because they were my window to a future different from what I experienced for the first 20 years of my life—a life lacking in resources. I encourage you to do the same, no matter what your situation is, and take a moment to write down your goals. This may not make a lot of sense right now, and you may not even have the courage or the energy to do so. That is why at this point in the story I am going to ask you to stop and write 25 goals you feel must be accomplished during your lifetime. Stop where you are and begin writing them now.

PRIORITIZE YOUR GOALS

My humble beginnings made the completion of my long-term goals even sweeter, but the greatest challenge was having the discipline to take those first small steps and begin the work. This is not comfortable, and it won't get better as time goes by, but it is essential. Your goals should be your priority every morning. Setting and working toward small, consistent, daily goals will keep you on a steady track toward fulfilling long-term goals.

The smaller, daily goals are just as significant as your long-term goals. You should think of your daily goals as bridges connecting you to your long-term goals. Every step forward you take on that bridge by completing a daily task is a step closer toward achieving your dreams. To put it another way, setting and completing your daily goals is necessary to realizing your long-term goals.

When making your long-term goals, you should take the advice that billionaire Warren Buffett gave to his pilot, Mike Flint, about setting long-term goals.[1] Buffett asked Flint to write his top 25 career goals, then circle the top five. Buffett explained that the key to success is to focus all your energy and efforts on the top five goals and disregard the other twenty.

Remember those goals I asked you to write down? Go ahead and circle the five most important. Depending on what you do in life, this technique should also be used in setting your daily goals. Establishing priorities, especially when it comes to your daily goals, is the key to propelling you toward a more successful life because it helps you stay focused on what is important. Prioritizing your goals also helps you identify trivial activities that do not contribute any value to your life and should be avoided at all cost.

---

1. Clear, J. Warren Buffett's "2 List" Strategy: How to Maximize Your Focus and Master Your Priorities. Retrieved from: https://jamesclear.com/buffett-focus

THE 5 SECOND RULE

When it comes to taking action to accomplish your long-term and short-term goals, I often refer to the 5 *Second Rule*, created by Mel Robbins.[2] She explains that each time you have a new idea, or anytime you are thinking of doing something important, you should count down from 5 (5-4-3-2-1) and take action, just like a rocket launch countdown from NASA. While this idea sounds almost too simplistic, it can be beneficial in combatting procrastination because it forces you to take action even when you don't feel like it... like when you're getting up in the morning.

Another concept from the 5 *Second Rule* is that your brain is at its peak learning capacity during the first two hours after waking up in the morning. You may have heard that successful people are often early risers who wake up hours before dawn every morning and go to bed early. The feeling of working on your most important life goal and preparing for your day before six in the morning will energize you for the rest of your day.

Example goals checklist items, as explained by the 5 *Second Rule* by Mel Robbins (more on that later):	
0400	Wake up time. Just count "5-4-3-2-1, and stand up."
0400-0500	Work on your life's highest goal.
0500-0515	Plan your day and prioritize the five things you need to accomplish for that day.
0515-0600	Professional reading. Reading about whatever you do that provides you the money to put food on your table.
0600-0630	Exercise. Exercise will provide you the energy needed to help decrease stress in your life.
Every evening	Write five things you were grateful for during your day.

2. Robbins, M. *The 5 Second Rule.*

GOALS BEFORE GOLD

While it might be possible that you do not accomplish some of your goals on a particular day or even within a particular year, you should never be discouraged in their pursuit. Putting in everything you have and giving it your very best will bring you that much closer to realizing your goals. If you fail, you can take comfort in knowing you have given it everything you have. Then, you will have a clear picture of what does not work and what to avoid in the future.

It is unlikely that you will succeed if you are too afraid to do what is necessary to transform your desires into reality. Without trying your best to realize your goals, you will not be any different than those who spend their life playing the lottery waiting and wishing to get lucky. You are not such a person, and you can create your luck, carve out your destiny, and shape your future. I will further say you *must* create your destiny. You were created for a purpose. Your desires will give you a glimpse or show a flicker of what that purpose is. You must transform that flicker of light into a raging fire that you can feel, breathe, and see in your mind. That fire will shine in your life, and you will serve as an inspiration to others who are starting off from the same place as you.

It is important to remember that, even in the rare instance that you do not reach your goals despite your greatest desires and arduous work, you would have never known that it was impossible until you tried. Also remember, "You will always miss 100% of the shots you don't take," so keep shooting at the dartboard of opportunity until you hit the center. You have probably heard, "Anything the human mind can conceive and believe, it can achieve"[3] by Napoleon Hill. There is wisdom in that quote, and when moving forward, you should regard that as fact and believe at your core that you can achieve all the desires of your heart. This may be difficult at first, but

---

3. Napoleon Hill. *Think and Grow Rich.*

if you truly do believe and have faith that you can achieve anything, you will always give 100%.

If you believed that everything we can conceive can be achieved, what goals would you set for yourself? Would they be any different from the goals I asked you to write earlier? Would they be goals that focused solely on improving yourself, or would they focus on humanity as a whole? If anything were possible just by conceiving it, what would you consider becoming? The simple truth is that yes, indeed, everything is possible, from the simplest to the most complicated ideas, thoughts, and dreams that you have ever had. All you have to do is set goals and take daily action toward the realization of these goals. It is that simple, as long as you remain committed to these daily actions.

Your life will continue to be as hard as it has been in the past if you don't adjust and make changes now. You didn't do the goal setting you needed to build a more successful life then, so you are where you are now. Even worse, it will be that much harder in the future if you do not set these goals now, take daily action toward their realization, and remain committed to them. If you keep doing the same thing and expecting a different result, you're going to drive yourself crazy! The above example is not to make light of such an important principle, but it is really that simple.

The Alchemist by Paulo Coehlo empowers readers, in a sense, to acknowledge that they are the creator of their future.[4] This is power, and the lack thereof is why so many people fail to achieve their highest potential in life. Think of your desires as metals that, only through the pursuit of your goals and by taking action, you can turn into results. It takes real effort to believe that nothing is impossible and to live every day with the confidence that is it just a matter of time before you achieve your goals. In his book, *Think and Grow Rich*, Napoleon Hill emphasizes that the simple fact that you can

---

4. Coehlo, Paulo. *The Alchemist.*

think about a dream or a goal is proof enough that you can realize it. If you can visualize it, you can achieve it.

Remember, sometimes life just happens and at times you need to be flexible. Flexibility does not mean you should not try your hardest and outwork everyone around you to achieve your goals. Flexibility means that sometimes greater opportunities or misfortunes will present themselves, and you should be flexible enough to recognize them and adjust accordingly.

Success takes time. First, you must have the desire to become successful. Luckily, most of us already have the desire for success built into who we are. We do want to be more successful and—equally as important—we want those around us and humanity in general to be more successful. The way to start becoming more successful is by first identifying what you want. You have to write down all your goals to bring forth that success. These goals should be the top five of the 25 goals you came up with earlier. The more significant and important these goals are to you, the better, because those goals will energize you more when you complete them.

Again, it is important to pick only the five most important goals, then break those five long-term goals into many small, daily tasks. You should ideally do them the first two waking hours of your day, and they should all go directly toward the accomplishment of those five goals. Next, practice waking up early; my suggestion is to wake up at four o'clock in the morning.

Success only comes from the efforts and the hard work that you put toward the realization of your goals. For example, after a couple hours of studying, you can earn good grades. After a couple of years of studies, you then earn your degree. After you complete your degree, you can use it to get a higher paying job. Just like a farmer, only after long days of preparing the land, planting, and watering can you reap what has been sowed. These examples can go on and on but remember that there is always a price to be paid in effort and hard work before you can achieve the success you desire.

Most of us never think about the effort, hard work, or sacrifices necessary to succeed, but they exist. How many practice shots did your favorite basketball player take for each successful shot in a game? There is no other way: You will have to work hard and outwork those around you before you can become successful. The only secret is to dedicate and focus your efforts on achieving your top five goals. The passion that you have will provide you with the energy and enthusiasm to do the work and to endure the sacrifices necessary to outperform everyone around you. This enthusiasm will also be what will sustain you to wake up while others are sleeping, stay up working long after others have gone to bed, persevere when others are defeated, and maintain your integrity when others are willing to compromise or sell their souls.

THE POWER OF GOALS

Many successful people can recall an opportune moment or circumstance when great opportunities simply appeared in their lives. The only way they can explain it is luck, as if their subconscious mind, the universe, the creator, God, or whomever they believe in helped them. I once heard someone compare this to something that happens to all of us when we drive. You might recall a time when you were driving from your house to work and somehow didn't recall a particular portion of the trip—as if that span of time never happened. The fascinating thing is that if you were ever involved in a car accident, it would only take a split second for that accident to occur. The question then is how can you drive safely when your conscious brain is not even aware of certain parts of your drive? Good luck alone does not explain that.

It is as if your subconscious mind, knowing that your goal is to go from your house to work supports your deliberate actions during your drive to get you to your final destination. Goals also serve the same purpose in our life. Your goals will do the same for you; they will bring opportunities in your path or bring people into your life who are willing to help you. People in the raging river of life will lock hands to help you cross safely to the other side. If you have difficulties understanding this concept, I encourage you to check out the resources below.

Unfortunately, most people only realize this concept after the fact—at the end of their careers when reflecting back on their lives. Understanding this concept will help you eliminate a large part of the self-doubt and pessimism that plague so many people. You'll have the confidence to move forward in your quest for a more successful life knowing that it is just a matter of time before your success is realized. And such knowledge will fill your anticipatory heart with joy instead of anxiety, hope rather than despair.

THE HARDSHIP OF HAVING GOALS

I wish I could tell you that all the steps you will be taking toward the realization of your goals will be easy, that you will never have a setback, that you will never be discouraged, and that you will never be tempted to give up. The sad truth is that you will face despair at many points in your life. At times you will be willing to give up. Maybe you have already given up in the past. I cannot tell you it will be easy because most of the time it isn't, but if your desires and passions are strong enough, and these goals are worthy to humanity and important enough to you, you will find the strength to endure. Everyone soon realizes that their attitudes toward these setbacks can make a big difference in helping them through moments of despair. In his book *See You at the Top,* Zig Ziglar explains that failures are only setbacks as long as you don't give up on your dreams. We should view setbacks as steps of a staircase leading us to the realization of our goals.

During one of the lowest points in my life, someone I looked up to told me, "The setbacks may seem insurmountable, but if you persist through them, you will one day look back to them as some of your proudest moments and would not want to change a thing about the tough times." I must admit, after hearing these words, I did not believe such a day would ever come. But now, looking back ten years later, I can sincerely say she was right.

These setbacks have brought me the confidence of knowing that tough times will pass. They have brought me the confidence of knowing anything is possible. As corny this may sound, I do believe this will also be the case for you. One day, when you look back at your past struggles and challenges, you will be proud of them. Most importantly, you'll thank God for helping you get through them, because what you will realize is that you are stronger for what you've endured. Think back on one of your darkest moments and the lessons you learned from that challenging time: I hope you can indeed see how you are now better for it.

Shawn Achor in his TEDx talk entitled "The Happy Secret to Better Work"[5] teaches you that remaining enthusiastic during struggles is a practice of gratitude. At the end of each day, take a few minutes to think about some of the things you are grateful for. We all have something that we can be thankful for, whether something small or very significant. If you ever think you have nothing to be grateful for, think again. Consider this idea in Mel Robbins's TED talk: The likelihood of your parents giving birth to you from your conception was 1 in 400 trillion. While the number may be different depending on the source, the point is still as blunt. You are a miracle to start with!

Also, consider the fact that you're alive while someone else is likely dying at this very second. Think of the fact that you can easily take a breath on your own, when so many who live with chronic lung disease may be gasping for air as you read. Think of the fact that you are free to do what you want while others are being tortured and oppressed in other parts of the world. While you are at it,

---

5. Shawn Achor at TEDx Bloomington.

also think how lucky you are to be reading a book with the potential to change your life while others may have already given up hope of a better tomorrow. The good thing is you can channel this gratitude into persistence. You have things to be thankful for! You can take action because you do indeed have many things to be thankful for.

REMAIN ENTHUSIASTIC

Another good way to maintain the energy needed to obtain your goals is to find a way to develop happiness from your goals. In his TED talk, Shawn Achor explains how people can derive happiness from gratitude. I will summarize the key point for you in this section, but I encourage you to dig deeper and listen to his TED talk. Before you go to bed each night, write down three things you are most grateful for. Alongside that, exercise each day for about 30 minutes. Instead of checking your email several times a day, check your email once a day in the morning after your exercise routine. Try also writing a grateful email to thank or praise someone who supports you. My suggestion is to start by sending this daily email to the person closest to you first. What you will come to realize is that in the same way your heart rate increases and your muscles tense when you think of a very negative and traumatic event, your physiology also changes when you focus on grateful events and express gratitude to others.

Information on how to achieve your goals is vastly available, but the biggest challenge you will face will be the difficulty of changing your previous habits. Your previous habits are what will prevent you from trying to develop your goals and work toward them. Maybe those habits are so strong that you consciously or subconsciously are too afraid to try the unknown. While you may have many different reasons to hold back, Anthony Robbins states that human beings ultimately default to doing things to either avoid pain or to get pleasure. I am sure you can think of many moments when this was true for you. Sometimes even though we know the pain and the fear we are going through, we are still unable to bring ourselves to make enduring changes and stick to our goals. Even though you may know that some particular actions (e.g., eating less if you're overweight) will bring great pleasure and success in the end, we sometimes do not take action and we miss out on that opportunity. What it boils down to is that your fears, former habits, and your insecurities are all holding you back.

There is no magic bullet that will change your habits in an instant either. You need to accept the fact it has taken you years to develop these habits, and it will likely take time and effort to break them. My advice is that you find the courage needed to realize your goals by focusing on the things you are grateful for in life and by visualizing the realization of your goals. Allow me to illustrate. Let us say that your goal is to become a physician. You may start by putting in some hard work on your studies. You'll soon see a positive change in your grades and you'll be thankful. Keep working! Start visualizing yourself as a physician. Have the picture of the physician you admire the most on a wall. Visualize yourself taking care of your patients in your mind. The truth is the more precise and detailed your written goals are and the more often you visualize them, the more likely you are to find yourself five to ten years later taking care of actual patients in your clinic.

You may find many ways to justify your success, just like you could have found so many reasons to justify your failure when you were not willing to start working at your goals. The truth of the matter is that when you are laser-focused on your goals and willing to outperform everyone around you, you will come to realize that the universe and your subconscious mind will bring opportunities to your life to help you accomplish your goals. Again, many times you will not be able to explain and justify how you have achieved these goals. You need to believe in your core that it is a fact of life that you will always be able to achieve your goals, provided that they are intended to do good in your life and the lives of those around you. And, secondly, you must be willing to pay the price of hard work.

First, having written your goals on a piece of paper that you can see and feel instead of just keeping them in your mind, you've taken your first step in building a more successful future. Second, you also now know that starting to work toward your goals on a daily basis will be difficult. Just like any new habit, writing down your goals and religiously working toward their realization will be difficult, but this new habit will eventually be as natural to you as breathing. Third, you have learned to prioritize your goals from your 25 lifelong goals to just the top 5. These five most significant goals, as Warren Buffett recommended to his pilot, should be the sole focus of your existence. You should live and breathe for their realization. Fourth, you have also learned about the power of goals. As you start pursuing your goals, you will realize that many opportunities will suddenly come to your life and things will start falling into place—just like the picture of a puzzle beginning to emerge. Fifth and finally in this chapter, you have learned about the importance of remaining thankful and enthusiastic. In everything that you do, show energy and be excited about it!

Having *goals* for your life was the first of the seven checklist items to create the more successful life you desire. Now you are about to learn about the second item in your checklist: taking action. While conceiving and writing your goals down is the best start you can hope to have, if you don't take action, they won't be worth anything more than the paper you wrote them down on! Taking action is what will breathe life into your goals. Let's go!

CHAPTER 2
TAKE ACTION ✔

Pledge to take action on every intuition and idea you conceive in your mind about your goals during the day. Apply *The 5 Second Rule* by Mel Robbins to take instant action on every goal-related idea that comes to your brain. Your subconscious mind is always working to bring ideas, opportunities, and people to your life to help with your goals. Act on these intuitions; they are the voice of your subconscious mind.

I know that not all of us can completely dedicate our life toward our true passion suddenly. But we can all devote the first two hours of our day toward the pursuit of our highest ideal. Why the first two hours of your day, you might ask? The first two hours of your day is when you have the most control. All you have to do is to wake up. No one expects you to be up at 4 a.m. to answer their phone calls or emails or interact with them on social media. Those first two hours are yours to keep for yourself, and you should be constantly using them to your advantage. Start by taking action each day of your life to wake up at 4 a.m. It will not be easy, but don't forget to do your countdown (5-4-3-2-1) and get started! The key, again, is to *take action*.

Avoid the temptation of delaying and waiting until you have time to take significant action. When it comes to achieving your goals, continuous and consistent daily actions are the best ways to proceed. How do you do that? If you go back to the top five most important goals you created in chapter 1, for each of these goals you should write 25 ideas on how to achieve those goals. Then, of course, discard all but five. Those five are your best bet to achieve success.

If you have trouble coming up with 25 ideas, you can obtain them from reading books on the topic of the specific goal, watching YouTube videos on the topic, or by reading and listening to interviews of the top five leaders in the areas of your top five goals. Seek to find out what five specific strategies these top leaders have applied to achieve their success. By the time you finish, you will recognize some overlap among the answers from your top five experts. What you need to do is pick the five most repeated answers. In the rare case that you didn't find any repeated answers, pick the five that are more consistent with your goals. Please remember you have to do that for each of your five goals.

My recommendation is to work toward the realization of your most important goal first. The one you believe is the most pressing is what you need to be focusing on most during the day. You need to work on it for the first of the two hours in the morning dedicated toward your goals and make it a constant priority. During the second hour, you will plan for your day, which also includes aspects of your other four goals.

Take action to write down all the things you want to accomplish in this life and then, from those goals, pick the most important five. Take action and start waking up early and dedicate the first two hours of your life each morning toward the achievement of these five goals. Take action to consistently do the things that contribute the most toward the realization of those five goals.

THE GPS OF SUCCESS

In the previous chapter, we discussed the importance of writing down your goals. You were also exposed to the simple truth that even the greatest and noblest goals will be insignificant in the long term if you don't take action toward their realization. Throughout this chapter, I will explain the steps of taking action toward achieving your goals. As I said earlier, this book will not be an easy promise of instant transformation, but rather a guide that will help you achieve your highest potential and show you the steps you need to take to get what you want in life.

By now you understand that goals are like the GPS in your car. GPS cannot fulfill its task unless you first enter an address that leads to your destination. A to-do list is just like a GPS that guides you from point A to point Z. You must start with a to-do list. Begin with the most important task of your day to the least. One thing that helps me toward achieving my goal is to wake up two to three hours earlier every day and work on my goals. Take yourself seriously; you owe it to yourself. Success is only ten percent intention and ninety percent action. Therefore, stop talking the talk of success and walk the walk instead. You already know your goals! Now is the time to set goals and start moving by taking deliberate actions every single day. Goals must be specific and achievable. For example, the goal of becoming president of the United States when you are a naturalized citizen is not an achievable goal, even though it is specific, because this is not allowed under the US constitution. Just like saying that you want to be wealthy is not specific because what is considered wealthy for one person may just be a month's expenses for another. Your goals should be tailored to you, based on your aspiration and the amount of effort you are willing to put forth to bring them to reality. There's no such thing as too little of a goal or too big of a goal. That is why you break them down into short- and long-term goals. Do not be complacent, either. You should write them down and give yourself time to accomplish them. Take one step at a time and do something every day toward your goal, and that will put you ever closer toward your success.

Please understand that I talk about moving toward your destination of a more prosperous life; this doesn't mean moving toward your *final* destination of success. This is because success is a continuum; there is no final point. Just like the GPS, even though we may have a set destination temporarily, soon we will move toward a farther destination. There will always be more to learn, more to improve on, more needs in the world, and more ways to help others. Sadly, if you work toward your success for years and you decide to stop, dissatisfaction will immediately set in. Learn from those who have made that mistake before you and persevere in your quest for a more successful life.

DO UNTO YOURSELF AS YOU WOULD UNTO OTHERS

People are usually willing to take actions and do things for their family, job, and friends more than they are willing to do things for themselves. It seems counterintuitive to human nature, but we observe it all the time. Parents will often make many sacrifices and take jobs to provide for their children that they would not take otherwise. Employees may be willing to wake up at 4 a.m. to go to work but are not willing to wake up that early to read a book or do something that would help them move toward the realization of their goals. A friend may be ready to drive a few hundred miles to visit a friend in need when he is not willing to attend a seminar or do anything to enhance himself.

Before I joined the United States Navy, I heard the saying, "In the Army, we do more by 9 a.m. than most people do in one day." I did not understand that concept at that time; in my mind, it was impossible to do more from 4 a.m. to 9 a.m. (i.e., in five hours) than most people do from 8 a.m. to 4 p.m. (eight hours). After my first day of Officer Development School (ODS) in Newport, Rhode Island, however, the answer was clear to me. Let me begin by saying that I was the first in my family to join the military, and worse, I did not do any research to know what to expect. I know you are likely thinking the same thing I am thinking writing this: that was dumb. And I concur with you. Yet that is a thing of the past now. I persevered.

That first day at 4 a.m., I heard a loud banging noise on my door and shouts of, "Wake up! Wake up!" My roommate, a former enlisted Marine, was already dressed in his exercise gear and ready to go. I asked him what was going on and he whispered, "Put your sneakers on, we are about to start." I was so scared and unprepared that first day. After that, I vowed to myself to be ready by 3:45 every day until the end of the training period. I learned my first lesson in the military that day, which was to "always be ready 15 minutes early and always be prepared."

I also learned something about group mindset. We are sometimes willing to do things or make sacrifices for our bosses that we are not willing to do for ourselves. Now think about this for a moment: A Navy Senior Chief Petty Officer whom I had never met before banged on my door at 0400, and I had to wake up. It wasn't just me who had to wake up, either, but all of the officer candidates. We had to comply to not only waking up at 0400, but we also all agreed to comply with every requirement of the training period. I had never experienced anything like that in my life before. From that experience, I learned to do for myself on a daily basis what that Senior chief expected of me—except now I am not doing it for the Senior Chief, I am doing it for myself. Are you willing to also do the same for yourself? Instead of doing your best to meet the expectations of the authority figures around you, how about you do your best to meet your own expectation of excellence—if only because you care and deserve nothing less.

The Senior Chief controlled us and treated us like sheep. Needless to say, we responded as obediently as any fearful and self-respecting group of sheep would. If the Senior Chief said left, we turned left and brought hell down to any poor soul who would dare to do otherwise. Think about this for a moment: if the choice were left up to us, I am afraid to say that very few of these motivated young professionals would wake up at 4 a.m. and learn as much as we had learned and achieved the same level of physical fitness as we had during that same time frame if it had just been themselves. The big question is, when it comes to personal achievements, are we willing to wake up and be ready to work so efficiently for ourselves? Why are we not so inclined to make the same sacrifices to achieve our personal goals? I will let you answer this question for yourself, but for me the answer is: If I did it for the Navy, I can, I must, and I will do it for myself. After all, I owe it to myself.

Do you feel the same?

If your answer is yes, I take it from this point forward you are committed to waking up at a time that allows you to diligently work on yourself each and every day.

YOU ARE YOUR OWN CEO

Consider the list below as the list of the top nine greatest companies in the world, listed by their function, but in no specific order. Company 1 produces the greatest transportation method on earth and is much more innovative and efficient than Tesla. Its vehicle can even run 18 hours without recharging. Company 2 is the greatest air filtration company in the world and can instantly filter down polluted air, load to the transport vehicles, and then immediately send its purified air out to all the places where it's needed. Company 3 is the greatest food processing company in the world. It does not process just meat but all kinds of foods with minimal waste by-products. Company 4 is the most efficient plumbing company in the world. About 98% of fluids passing through it are reusable. Company 5 is the most sophisticated production line company. Its different parts move with great precision, are coordinated, and can perform a diverse range of motions. Each one of its extension responds as a faithful servant to every command of the company owner. Company 6 is the most sophisticated pharmaceutical company in the world. Its drugs are highly efficacious with no side effects. Company 7 is the most efficient water pump and purification company in the world. The pipes of the unit go to every corner of the city it services. At its lower range of function, it cycles about 86,000 times per day and can keep going for years without needing any form of external power. Company 8 is the biggest computer company in the world, more valuable than Apple and Microsoft combined. Company 9 is the most sophisticated clothing company. Its garments provide ample protection and repair themselves in case they are accidentally torn.

Before you say such companies do not exist, think with me for a moment. If you were an employee of any one of these companies, what kind of employee would you be? Would you wake up at 4 a.m. and start your day so you can be in the office by 7:45 a.m. until the end of shift at 4 p.m? Would you be happy to do that five to seven days a week, and wouldn't you be even more pleased if you were allowed to work overtime? Would you have faith that any one of these companies would take care of you as their employee? How proud would you feel to tell people that you work for one of these top nine companies?

Now, what if I were to tell you that each one of these companies represented here is one of your nine organ systems and that you are not just a mere employee of just one of them, but you are the CEO of all nine of them combined? Go back and read them again and identify all nine of the "companies" knowing that they are nine individual organ systems. You need to think and believe in yourself as the most important person in the world that you are—a miracle. Take the same type of action you are willing to take for your daily job because you are that much more valuable. The compensation will be so much more lucrative, and the satisfaction you will gain will be so much more rewarding and long lasting.

TAKING EFFECTIVE ACTIONS

If actions are worth taking and if hard work has to be performed, it should be done as effectively as possible. Just like other successful people, you will come to the realization that your most precious resources are the 24 hours that you have been granted each day. It is essential to understand and keep the value of these 24 hours in mind whenever you take action. You should plan carefully each day to take effective action and make the most out of that time.

The same is true about working hard and not letting anyone outwork you. While you are working hard toward the realization of your goals, you should also work efficiently. Your goal should not only be to become the guy that no peer can out-work, but also to be the most efficient among your peers. For example, you should seek to correlate your hard work and efficiency in term of the value you create for your customers or your employers. When you find ways to create more value through your determined attitude and efficient mindset, you'll be in demand; you will be indispensable, and, by default, you will be on the fastest route to success possible.

While your current job may not be ideal for you, and you may be obliged to keep it because you need the money, you should still not stop wanting to do something better. Remember, always strive to be the leader you would want to follow; strive to be the calm voice in the midst of the chaos, and—while you are at it—strive to be the change that you want to see. And let me ask you, what kind of boss wouldn't want to hire such a professional as you? I know I would.

Always do more than what you get paid to do; this is how you make yourself valuable. Never take action for the sake of going through the motions; be purposeful and goal-oriented. You should always demand of yourself the very best you have, then go above and beyond. You need to understand what you are reading here is not for everyone, just like not everyone around you is successful nor wants to be successful. Success in life takes effort and sacrifice. The only thing that will sustain and stimulate you throughout the long hours, the pain, the heartbreaks, the despair, the disappointments, and the setbacks is your passion.

If you act as if it were impossible to fail, while remaining truly passionate about your desires and your goals, you will always succeed. If, for some reason, you were to decide to abandon that endeavor before it could come to fruition, what you will learn from trying and giving your best shot will nevertheless be valuable. This is indeed a win-win situation.

SUCCESS IS LIKE SWIMMING AGAINST THE CURRENT

Success in life is like swimming against the current. Just like the salmon swimming against the current in Ketchikan, Alaska, you will find that taking action may be uncomfortable and risky. Yet taking action is crucial if you do not want to be swept away by the current of life. What you will also find important is the sheer amount of vigor the salmon in Ketchikan have when they swim. If you pay close attention, you will notice that they do not swim timidly thinking they may or may not make it, and they are not trying to play it safe like most people do. They don't focus on trying not to lose everything in case they don't make it. Instead, they give it everything they've got. They give it all, poised as if success were guaranteed.

Of course, we know that they must be aware of the challenges they face during such a journey, but does that stop them from achieving what they were born to do? No. They face the challenges of not only extreme exertion, but also the dangers of being caught by the bears or the fishermen waiting on the shore. Their mom, dad, or cousins have likely told them, "Don't you think such a journey is dangerous?" I am sure they may have probably heard of fellow salmon that did not make it.

You have probably also heard such negativity in the news today; it turns out that bad news sells better than good news. At this point in your life, you too may already be exposed to the challenges of success, either through personal shortcomings or from the challenges those around you have been through. You have probably seen your parents and loved ones giving their best constantly when they saw no way out.

The key to success in life is to take action and keep moving forward with confidence as if you cannot fail. Many people do not achieve the success they so desire in life because they fail to understand that being successful at anything requires significant sacrifice—more sacrifice than you care to read on these pages, or I care to list. At the end of the day, no matter how hard you will have to work or the number of sacrifices that you will have to make if you are genuinely passionate about your desires, your goals, and your passion, all the sacrifices will not stop you from achieving your goal.

In fact, you will find yourself saying at the end that all the sacrifices have been well worth it and if you had to do it all over, you would not change a thing. The key is to write your goals and focus on the things you think you want to do in life very carefully. If you are not wildly passionate about your goals, the struggles you will have to face in the course of achieving any worthwhile goal may make your goal undesirable. If the passion is not there, the challenge may become insurmountable and eventually may force you to give up or may cause you to experience great dissatisfaction, even if you are eventually successful. Such a victory will be many times harder than it would have been if passion were the foundation of your endeavor.

Again, the key is to keep doing your best every day, day in and day out. I strongly doubt if God, The Almighty, and The Creator of the Universe would have put the desire to be successful in your heart if He did not know beforehand that you had it within you to achieve it.

ADVERSITY IS THE IMPETUS FOR ACTION

Parents often say they don't want their kids to go through the same struggles they went through in life, or they don't want their kids to struggle at all. Some proudly say that the reason they work so hard is so their children will not have to later. While most people may not regard adversity as a blessing in disguise until after they have achieved their success in life, the truth is that every successful person you get to know will describe their adversities as some of their greatest blessings. Adversity helps develop your character and helps us to remain humble and realistic while still pushing us to succeed.

The job of any good checklist is to prepare you to avoid common dangers, so that is the job of this book. You may not agree with the fact that one day you will consider your adversities to be your greatest blessings, but the job of these seven checklist items is to prepare you for these truths.

Consider, for a moment, if your mother were very wealthy and had promised you the car of your dreams the day you turned 20. How much would you work for this car? Probably not very much. If Arnold Schwarzenegger were shown in a dream that he would be the greatest bodybuilder of his time and decided he did not need to go to the gym because of that, do you think his muscles would have developed on their own? Just like muscles need the constant challenges and adversities posed to them by weights to develop, so do you to be successful in life.

Adversities challenge you to develop into the best version of you. You will probably agree that if a young individual has a mental attitude fueled by passion and action, she is destined for a more successful life—despite whether or not she has had a supposed prophecy. You must believe within your core that if God promises you something by putting His desires in your heart, if you then transform those desires to goals and then take action, it is just a matter of time before you achieve them. The desires would not have been placed in your heart if you did not have all that you need within you to achieve them.

LEARN FROM YOUR CRITICS

You have likely already noticed that life is complex, and to say there are many grey areas and misconceptions in life is a fair statement. People may be upset and criticize you for having big goals and taking action to realize them. The critics will say this is impossible; you are too ambitious, and you don't have what it takes. They will throw anything at you.

While it might seem impossible for a poor kid living in the poorest country in the western hemisphere to say he wants to study to become a nurse, a lawyer, a physician, or a teacher in another country with some of the most advanced academic programs in the world, continuous small action and studying and learning with passion may fuel him to create the link between his desires and their realization.

Whereas the critic may view the idea of continuous improvement in achieving one's utmost ideal or success a recipe for dissatisfaction, the truth remains that there are many things in life that can lead to the feeling of dissatisfaction. Not the least of them is the feeling of complacency from past successes. Quite often, the truth lies within the grey areas.

In my experience, I have found that psychologists and psychiatrists are the keenest to appreciate and explain these nuances. Unfortunately, I don't have these skills and you probably don't either; suffice it to say that things are not always what they seem. The key point for you, then, is always to be willing to listen to your critics and learn from them—especially in times when those grey areas may exist. Remember you don't have to agree with them and you shouldn't let their voices stop you from pursuing your goals, but you can always learn from them.

Once you start taking actions toward realizing your goals, you should remember that there will be people who find reasons to criticize you for many things. What you will notice is that many critics may have the best intentions in mind. They may simply fundamentally disagree with you, and that is okay; we are all different and our experiences are as diverse as we are as individuals. Again, you should seek to learn from your critics because they may be presenting you with a different perspective that you have not considered. What you should never allow yourself to do, however, is to give up on your desires and goals because of critics—as long as your desires and goals will not cause unintended harm to you or others. By giving up, you give them the power over you.

In your journey to success, taking action is the engine of your more successful life which is fueled by the passion that will push you forward toward your success. Just like your goals, your actions should always be guided by truth, integrity, and the intention to do good to yourself and others. What you will come to realize over and over again is that those actions will not always be easy or popular, but if they are taken and are acted upon with the best of intentions, you will always be able to weather the storm of criticism that is most likely going to come your way.

I once heard someone say that having people criticize you is a good thing. It is a sign that you are up to something good, something that is worthy of being criticized. I am sure that you will not always feel this way when you are on the receiving end of criticism, but you heard it here first.

The best remedy to criticism is taking action. You have already learned in this book about the amazing power of setting daily short-term goals and the importance of taking small, daily actions to realize them before you go to bed each day. Small, consistent actions have the accumulative effect of compound interest: What seems to be insignificant at first, over time has very powerful effects.

While many may think they are powerless to do the work required for achieving their goals, you know now that this is not true. You should always break your goals into small, daily, achievable goals, which serve as steps from your desires to the realization of your ultimate success in life.

During the course of your day, whenever it is time to take action, whether you want to or not, commit yourself to follow through by following the 5 Second Rule of Mel Robbins (5-4-3-2-1 ACTION). Always remember that the realization of small, daily goals is like placing an individual brick in the construction of your ultimate successful life.

In case you have ever wondered, the distance between your goals and their realization can be shortened by taking action. Remember taking action should always be decisive (5-4-3-2-1 ACTION) and with the best intentions in mind.

If you are asking why the same idea has been repeated multiple times in this chapter, it is because we are talking about action. Actions are always repetitive until they become second nature; once they become second nature, you will keep repeating them effortlessly. This should be a goal for all of us.

TAKING ACTION LEADS TO A MORE PERFECT LIFE

The words from the first paragraph of the constitution of the United States, "To form a more perfect union," captivated my imagination when I first read it as a teenager living in Haiti, with the goal of one day coming to America. My anticipation was rooted in the hope that I could lead a better life in a place where I was surrounded by successful peers. The only thing standing in my way was the application for permanent residency and its approval.

My English was poor, and needless to say, I did not understand everything. But what I found fascinating about the constitution of the United States at that time—and even after all these years living in the United States—was the faith of the forefathers in a better future. Even though the constitution was written at the time of the infancy of the United States and its brightest future was likely beyond what anyone could have imagined at that time, the founders did not dwell on the challenges of their present situation. Instead, they focused on what was perfect in the union at the time when they wrote the constitution and contemplated the goals for a more perfect union.

They had the wisdom of knowing that perfection is not final. They understood that perfection has to be maintained and serviced routinely from the lessons learned from the past, mixed with an industrious present that paves a better road to the future, leading to a more perfect union. The forefathers willingly offered their shoulders of hope for future generation to stand on so that they could see further than they could have ever seen in their lifetime.

Their words, "In order to form a more perfect union," were their instruction to the future generation of Americans, of all creeds and backgrounds, to offer their shoulders so that the future generations could see even farther. While you may have a past full of challenges, setbacks, and fear, you may benefit from learning of the example set forth in the constitution of the United States by seeking to find the perfect thing in your current situation and take action to make it more perfect each day.

Many of us, at some point in our lives, will realize that the perfect life we have been seeking to the point of anguish leads us to say, "There is no perfection in life." But it's actually staring us in the face. Unfortunately, we have just never focused on it or paid attention to it. As you may imagine, you are unlikely to hit a target if you are not looking at it. That perfection in our life is all around us; it is our ability to think of a more perfect future, to see hidden opportunities, to feel the touch of a loved one, to breathe hope into the lives of others, and simply our ability to be alive.

Once you start to focus on your perfection, you will begin to realize that you are more perfect than you have ever imagined before and that the more perfection you aim for, the easier it will be to find. As a result, it will pave the road to your more successful life with more hope and opportunities. Finding perfection in your present circumstances will give you the strength to persevere, to move forward and see the big picture, and to learn to focus on what is important in life.

Such an understanding should encourage you to take action and to push you to attain and become your more perfect self. What most people fail to realize is that the perfect things or the perfect dreams in life we are seeking are all around us hiding in plain sight.

Instead of focusing on our passion or what we want, we are instead focused on what we don't want (e.g., debt, sickness, betrayal, lack of opportunities, etc.). Unfortunately, whatever you focus on is what you will get… it is really that simple.

A race car driver knows this, and that is the reason why she always keeps her eyes fixed on where she is going. The idea that there is no such thing as a perfect life or perfection in life is simply a lie. It is a lie that many of us have grown to believe because we focus on what we don't have and fail to appreciate and develop gratitude for what we do have.

It is up to you at this very moment to break the cycle of helpless dissatisfaction and shift your focus to what you are passionate about to see your life in a new light. It is your right and your obligation to see your life as a light shining on a more perfect tomorrow and radiating on relationships, prosperity, health, and a more perfect life for you and for those around you.

Moving forward, all you need to do to reach that perfect success in life is to take action. Moving forward, make the decision from now on to take action to continuously improve yourself to be a more perfect husband, wife, son, daughter, worker, or just a more perfect human being beaming with enthusiasm and impeccable integrity.

To illustrate this concept as it relates to the mental attitude of success in life, imagine you wanted to lose weight to have a more perfect body and enjoy better health. You know to take action right away and start your exercise regimen today. When you start to take action, it is easy to become impatient and ready for immediate results; indeed, most people feel this way.

While you seek a more perfect and successful life, you need to learn to be patient. The example of trying to lose weight is a good analogy in the sense that people sometimes tend to forget that the weight they seek to lose was slowly accumulated, maybe over the course of months to several years. They fail to realize that to lose that weight, they not only have to do the opposite of what they have done to gain the extra weight, but they should also allow themselves at least the same amount of time it took to gain the weight in order to lose it.

The same concept is true when it comes to developing a positive mental attitude for a more successful life. What you will notice over time is that you will start to develop a more positive view for your future, you will have stamina, and you will start enjoying pushing yourself beyond even your new limits. As long as you remain consistent with your daily actions toward self-improvement, you will likely lose the negative mental attitude of self-doubt and helplessness in, hopefully, less time it took you to accumulate it.

How much time exactly? you may ask. It depends on your action. Just like if you were trying to lose weight; how much weight you lose depends on the actions you take for exercising as advised by your doctor. The same idea is true when it comes to changing your mental attitude to a positive one and focusing on a more successful life. The key is to realize that you have to make an immediate decision to change, and this decision should be accompanied by immediate action continued daily until the new habit is developed or the changes you desire are obtained. There are indeed similarities and correlations between taking action toward our goals and the achievement of a more perfect, successful life. All you need to do is to see the perfection in the present and take action to make it even more perfect in the future.

TAKE ACTION ONLY AFTER SETTING DETAILED GOALS

This chapter on taking action cannot be completed without reiterating the importance of planning and establishing detailed goals before taking action. A running car will not take the driver anywhere until the gear is set to drive and the brakes are released. Actions without a detailed plan derived from your goals won't happen, either. Your goals should be the foundation for your actions.

Pause for a moment and think of some very busy people you know who are always on the go. It's likely that if you were to ask them what their goals are, you'd find that their actions are not consistent with those goals. If your goals were to save money to pay for your kid's college, but yet you are spending your money on expensive cars and luxurious vacations, you'd probably agree that such actions are not well-suited to achieving that goal.

The actions you take on a daily basis should be consistent with the five most important goals of your life. Think of it this way: Your actions are the results of your plans; your plans are derived from your goals, and your goals were derived from the five most important desires you want to accomplish in your quest to a more successful life. In short, your actions have to be consistent with your goals.

At this point, you have just checked off two of the *7 Checklist Items for Success*.

Goals ✔ and Taking Action ✔ .

Now, we will move to item number three, which is Courage.

CHAPTER 3

COURAGE TO CONSISTENTLY COMMIT

Have the courage to go the extra mile in everything that you do, each and every time. Never let yourself be outworked by anyone. Working hard is the greatest equalizer in life. Have the courage to remain enthusiastic and do everything with a smile on your face and a genuine desire to help and serve those around you. Have the courage to be flexible and adapt when the situation demands it. Have the courage to maintain your integrity at all costs. It takes years to develop a reputation for integrity, but all can be lost in an instant.

One common theme you may have noticed in this book is the cumulative effect of the small things over time. While it may be easy to recognize an act of courage when someone makes the ultimate sacrifice of giving his or her life to save someone else, smaller acts of courage are often left unrecognized by society. A firefighter who died after entering a flaming building to save a young child or a Marine who died after jumping on a grenade to save his comrades must surely have boundless courage. While such acts are correctly viewed as heroic, people often forget to comment on what causes heroes to take action when others would have likely frozen or run away from the dangers under the same pressure or circumstances.

The reason for this phenomenon likely has to do with training. Firefighters have trained arduously and run practices hundreds of times. Although the majority of their calls may be routine, they understand that their training can make the difference between life and death—not only for themselves, but also for the lives of those in danger. The same is true for the Marines Corps; they are very well trained and understand that their lives are intertwined with the lives of the other members of the team. Each of one of them is willing to give his or her life to save another team member.

While most of us don't have risky jobs like firefighters or members of the military, courage is as important for each one us as it is for them. While the courage of a firefighter is tested during each call he responds to, our courage instead is tested daily by our actions… albeit not to the same level of danger. During the course of our day, we can choose to act courageously by taking actions consistent with our goals, by forcing ourselves to abstain from procrastination, and to apply Mel's 5 Second Rule to help us to take action.

For the average person, it takes courage to remain enthusiastic in times of setbacks or uncertainty. It also takes courage to maintain our integrity and do the right thing in the face of temptations or when the difference between right and wrong may not be very well defined. The point to remember is that each time we choose to act courageously the fibers of our character are strengthened, putting us in a better position to act when it matters the most.

You may be faced with a decision whereby your action could mean the difference between setting valuable goals consistent to your highest ideals or to just following the path of least resistance. Those acts of courage are important because they are what will get you to act courageously when everything is on the line. In fact, when you take into account that no one is looking and that your brain is trying to talk you out of taking any action, these acts of courage are very significant.

You may want to take a sip of alcohol. While your brain is telling you this is not a big deal, each moment and each day you are able to refrain from that sip is an act of success whether it is noted by others or not. Such an act of success is especially significant when you have only been in recovery from alcoholism for a month after being addicted to alcohol for many years before. The truth is that it takes courage to resist this temptation and the temptations of whatever other forms of addiction you may be facing.

The true signs of courage are these small acts, because each one will build your confidence to act when everything is on the line. Have the courage to take daily action without hesitation, be tough, and act courageously. What you will eventually come to realize is that those moments that required courage usually do not last a long time, but courageous people persevere forever.

THE COURAGE TO MAKE A DIFFERENCE

At the end of chapter two, we talked about the importance of taking action on your quest to a more successful life. Well, it takes courage to fight the complacency. You need to remind yourself that, despite the fact it may take a lifetime to reach a more successful life, all can be lost in an instant if you don't show the courage to keep your integrity at all times.

The courage to be patient, the courage to inspire those around you, the courage to forgive, and the courage to keep moving forward even though we want to give up is the courage needed to make a difference. No matter how far you have reached in your current level of success, it is a fallacy to think that you have made it or that you are on top of the world. Despite your desire to kick back and relax, you need to keep moving forward and at the same time have the courage to look back and pull someone up with you, despite your fear of getting pulled back in the bucket of mediocrity or selfishness.

Have the wisdom and foresight to understand that the true purpose of your success is to improve lives, not only yours but also those around you. Love even though you have been the object of betrayal. Understand even though you have been misunderstood. Give even though you have been robbed before. Feed the hungry even though you have starved in the past.

The truth is, the strength of your courage and your character have helped you overcome your past challenges, and they will strengthen your courage to face future challenges. Have the courage to remain energized by your goals and to be passionate and diligent about them. Adjust to new situations and circumstances; life may not always turn out the way you want it.

There will be many times you may want an ice cream out of life, but life might hand you a lemon instead. You must be flexible enough to make lemonade if life hands you a lemon instead of complaining of its bitterness. Have the courage to remain committed to your goals to adapt, and—most importantly—the courage to uphold your integrity at absolutely all costs.

Such courage is not easy, but necessary to make a difference. You might come short sometimes, stumble, or even fall down from acting courageously. But please remember that, in life, it is not the number of times you fall that counts, but whether or not you have the courage to rise up again and brush the dirt off your back.

WHAT IS YOUR PRICE TO STOP?

Have the courage to keep your vision and your goals alive, even though those around you don't understand them or believe in you. At the beginning of his book *Good to Great*, Jim Collins opens by asking himself how much money someone would have to pay him to not write it. I asked myself the same question about this book when I first read the story.

The answer that arose was that absolutely no amount of money could stop me from writing this book. The answer to the question came to me a little too easily, so I stopped for a moment to think it through. The answer was still the same! It is funny how the right answers to some of the toughest questions come to us if we dare to ask them—or, most importantly, if we listen to our intuition and take a leap of faith to accept the meaning of the answers. Now let me ask you the same question: How much money would someone have to pay you to stop your quest for the discovery of a better you and a more successful life?

The realization that no amount of money would make me stop this project was the courage that showed me the value of this book does not dwell in monetary form, but instead in the value that it might one day improve someone's life. I sincerely hope that someone is you. I think most of us are going through life with the anticipation of finding a treasure and are seeking to get something for nothing, or maybe are seeking to get something for the least amount of effort possible, such as working for a paycheck from a job we don't like.

Perhaps we never have the courage to ask the real questions— and, most importantly, the courage to accept the answer. Because the truth is, if you are doing what you are passionate about or something you truly believe in, it is unlikely that any price would make you stop. If money can stop you, you may reach a point where you don't have the courage to go on, because the financial sacrifice to persist may not be worth the perceived value of your efforts.

The opposite is also true. If your desire to persist is priceless, you may be pleasantly surprised to discover that your courage to persevere is limitless. Your vision will widen when you choose to devote your time and talents to pursuing goals that are priceless. Let your passion be the judge of the value of the goals you seek to realize.

Creating a more successful life derives its true worth from the value it creates in the lives of others. The sense of worth that derives from pursuing worthwhile goals will undoubtedly lead to success. If wealth is what you are seeking for in life, it will undoubtedly be attained from pursuing goals that create value to others; all in all, wealth is only a by-product of the value that you create for others. The more value you create for others, the wealthier you will be; it is that simple.

Don't complicate this. The Bible clearly tells us that we reap what we sow. Not only is it a promise from God, but it is also a law of the universe. Every action is compensated for with an equal and opposite reaction when discussing force. When discussing humanity, often we are surprised to learn that the good deeds we do for others today can be reaped in the future at a ten-fold and even a hundred-fold return! In a nutshell, the value of investing in yourself via the value you create in the lives of others is directly proportional to the value you have created for yourself through self-improvement.

I chose to bet on you by deciding to write this book with the conviction that it would detail how to live a more successful life to anyone with a desire to achieve success. The information in this book goes beyond any monetary value, and I am committed to providing you the information that I believe would have made my own journey to a more successful life smoother.

I am convinced that you will not let me down. I know you will make a similar bet on yourself and commit to making every effort to finish this book—most importantly, to applying the seven checklist items for success in your life on a daily basis. I am looking forward to hearing your story.

THE COURAGE TO BE SUCCESSFUL IN LIFE

Unfortunately, sometimes we face setbacks and shortcomings despite our best efforts. I hope during such times your courage will provide you with the strength to move forward with renewed energy in the belief of a better tomorrow. The courage to go on is the type of benefit that can be gained from going through challenges and setbacks in life.

We sometimes fail to notice that our response to a setback can produce an outcome even more detrimental than the setback itself. For example, if an individual chooses to stop pursuing his goals after a setback, it is probably reasonable to think that such reaction may be more dangerous than the setback itself. Another person facing a similar setback who views her setback as a bump in the road or just as a step on the ladder to a more successful life will have a much greater chance at excelling later. Experience has taught us that the second individual will likely bounce back from her setback and continue to move toward her desired goals. Never fail to underestimate the human mind in terms of the interpretation we give to the situations in our lives. Those interpretations play a big role in how we continue to view life. It can be a vicious cycle.

I am afraid to say that if the forefathers of the United States had chosen to focus on the setbacks or ordeals that the United States had to face, or the sacrifices that its people had to make to gain their independence, this country would not be the beacon of hope that it has been for the world since its independence. The citizens of this country would have probably felt uncertain of their futures, and America as we know it today would likely be very different. Instead, the forefathers of that new country chose to focus on what was perfect. They encouraged their fellow citizens to keep moving toward a *more* perfect union.

Sometimes I wonder how our world would have been different if our parents were only to focus on what is perfect about their children and encourage them to be more perfect. I sometimes wonder how the world would be different if more teachers, in addition to the great good that they are already doing, were to focus on what is perfect about their students and encourage them to be more perfect. If employers were to focus more on what is perfect about their employees and encourage them to be more perfect, how would the workplace change? If a husband or wife were to focus more on what is perfect about each other and encourage each other to be more perfect, would America's staggering divorce rate be much lower than it is now? I sometimes wonder how much better it would be if more religious leaders were to focus more on what is perfect about their followers and encourage them to be more perfect. This is not a new concept; its proof of concept was tested in America in 1787 when the constitution was written.

The courage it will take to be successful in life is much greater than what many people believe or are willing to put forth. Most people say that they will do whatever it takes to be successful in life, but once they truly realize the courage it takes to follow something even as simple as these *7 Checklist Items for Success*, most of them fail to have the courage to continue. The strange thing is that even in the face of obvious lack of follow-through and of commitment to a defined plan, some, if not most, people will still talk the talk and say that they "gave their best." The sad thing is it that these people, in their minds, do not intend to lie or hide the facts. The truth is that they believe that they have done their best... even when the rest of us can clearly see how they have fallen short in so many instances (e.g., not setting goals, not waking up early to work on self-improvement, not remaining committed to any goal, not following a daily schedule or a daily to-do list, etc.).

Moving forward, whenever you are facing problems that seem insurmountable, in addition to asking yourself whether or not you have done your best, ask yourself if you have really done what needed to be done. Many times, instead of playing the mind game of thinking that you did your best, realize that what you really need to be doing is living on a friend's sofa while you are building that new business, waking up two hours earlier to work on achieving your personal goals, or simply committing to never giving up until success is reached no matter how many times you fall. Swear to yourself that you will always get up no matter how hard or painful it will be.

How about you commit to seeing that your marriage succeeds and that those around you feel loved? How about you commit to seeing that you never give up on that child or that person in your life who needs you? How about you commit to looking at yourself in the mirror every night and being absolutely certain that you have done your best with your God-given talent for that day.

Don't seek to take the easy road in life. The easy road is what causes many people to use so many other words in order to avoid the word "courage" because they know there is no courage in taking the easy road. They will say they were unsuccessful because they were unlucky, it was the wrong time, they are from a dysfunctional family, etc. Be careful whenever you are about to use the word "because" as it's likely the next few words that follow will be an excuse.

The truth is successful people are very courageous. They do not need to find excuses for their setbacks and you can be sure that, no matter what happens, they have done their best. Most importantly, they have learned from those setbacks for next time. Successful people show proof of courage each time they choose to set goals that seem bigger than their current situations, goals that stretch, goals that seem impossible to the critics.

And you better believe that when courageous people set goals, they are willing to endure all the sacrifices needed to succeed. The courage to succeed in life also means having the courage to avoid doing things that are not productive. This, I believe, is a key trait of successful people. The purpose of having goals in life is not just to focus your attention on what you want to accomplish, but also to focus your attention away from the nonproductive things you will certainly encounter and have to face on your journey to the realization of the more successful life you want.

The fact is, the things you should not do in order to be successful in life may take as much courage as the things that you have to do to be successful. For example, having the courage not to watch the evening news or your favorite TV shows may take the same amount of courage as dedicating that time toward working on your goals and self-improvement.

I am quite generous when I say it might be the same amount of time you may need to dedicate to your goals and self-improvement, because if you look at it closely, most people spend far more than two hours a day doing things that are unproductive. If anything, these unproductive activities have an inverse relationship toward achieving a more successful life. Doing unproductive things is, in a way, like overlooking what it takes to be successful. Meanwhile, your top five goals you want to accomplish the most in life or your to-do list may be only take a fraction of the time you waste doing things that are not part of your goals or dream.

You may find it surprising how much you can accomplish in one day if you avoid doing the things that are not important for your more successful life. It takes real courage to apply the previously mentioned reported advice Warren Buffett gave to his pilot. Once you decide on your five goals in life, avoid doing everything else that does not contribute toward these five goals. While Warren Buffet's advice is having worthwhile goals in life and the importance of avoiding things that do not contribute to our success in life, I think it does not go far enough to warn people against the numerous things that don't contribute to our success out there.

When considering the amount of time the average individual spends watching TV or surfing on social media, it is unlikely that they truly understand the importance of avoiding fruitless and mindless activities. Maybe the average person should set goals to remind them *not to do* those things that they know they should avoid. However, I think such a "not to do" list would be impractical because of the sheer amount of distractions that we all face in our life on a day-to-day basis.

Be cognizant of the fact that much of what you do during the course of your day is not consistent with your goals. How about you try to limit the amount of time you spend on social media, TV, or video games by half until you are ready to reduce them to less than 30 minutes per day? Better yet, how about you choose to just follow an exercise program instead of checking your email every 5 or 10 minutes? Have the courage to stop doing those things and instead do the things that matter to your more successful life.

BE GRATEFUL

Gratitude is the simplest way to develop a feeling of well-being. It is like most things in life, the more you think about gratefulness, the more grateful you will feel and the more grateful you will become. It is important to have the courage and discipline to write about five things you were most grateful for at the end of each day. If during your evening routine, you think of someone you are grateful for, don't forget the next day to call or email him or her to personally express your gratitude; people are always appreciative of such gestures.

Try to always be grateful and say thank you. It is up to you to find your own reason to be happy and grateful. Gratitude is by far one of the simplest ways to develop a sensation of happiness. In life, we will sometimes face a situation in which we may be hard-pressed to find reasons of gratitude, like the death of a loved one or a moment of despair. No matter what the situation may be, it is up to every one of us to find reasons to be grateful—even though we may be disappointed or despairing at the moment. You will come to realize that it is very difficult to harbor a feeling of gratitude and dissatisfaction at the same time.

GIVE OTHERS THE BENEFIT OF THE DOUBT

The human mind seems to, by default, dwell on worst-case scenarios when it comes to our dealings with other people. This is our brain's way of protecting us and reminding us to remain vigilant of our surroundings. Being always on guard was a survival skill during primitive years, but at present such a way of thinking is more a paranoia of getting duped or scammed.

You may be upset by others' actions that may be inconsistent with your goals or your own values. But remember giving others the benefit of the doubt can go a long way and can help you see other points of view. Try to put yourself in their shoes and always ask yourself (based on their level of consciousness, their cultural norms, and their values) whether or not you would have acted differently in the same situation.

Often, after giving people the benefit of the doubt, you will realize that they are decent people doing and acting the best they can based on their perception of the situation. The courage to give others the benefit of the doubt does not come easy; it requires both judgment and discernment, but the benefit to our well-being should not be underestimated.

The benefit of living a life free of grudges against others is tremendously liberating. When you are not sure, or you do not have the proof to support your doubts except for the fear in your mind, give the benefit of the doubt. If all the facts point to a certain conclusion, however, by all means you should accept the facts. If it looks like a duck, swims like a duck, and quacks like a duck, then it probably is a duck.

SHOW TO OTHERS A REFLECTION OF THEIR PERFECTION

It is common to look at the final stage of someone's life—which we can also call their more successful life—and say they are very lucky. We, for some reason, think it is just natural that person became successful. We think that the speech that the president of the United States gave at his inauguration was easy. We completely forget all the years of training dedicated to the art of public speaking and the skills of his speechwriting team. We also forget the many years of experience of the visual aids and the teleprompter team. We forget the many years of experience as a politician this newly elected president has accrued, and we may completely forget the speeches he had to give during his time in college as the president of various organizations. We completely forget about how much he has had to practice before the delivery of the perfect inaugural speech.

We think it is easy when we go to the doctor that just after a couple of minutes he can come up with the diagnosis for our signs and symptoms and promptly decide on a treatment plan for that medical ailment that been bothering us for weeks, months, and—in some cases—years without us figuring it out. The strange thing is that we completely forget about the many years of study. We forget the rigorous four years of grueling medical school and the 3-5 years of residency training when the doctor worked over 80 hours a week in the hospital, not including personal study time, with a yearly pay of about $40,000 while having a family to support. We forget by the time we sit in front of this doctor in the clinic that she is the product of at least 11 years of intense post-secondary study.

Many other examples can be given, but these will suffice for now. When we look at this newly inaugurated president or that physician in the clinic, we don't think of the courage those people of high aptitude have displayed through countless repeated small acts on a daily basis over the course of their career without us never knowing about them. And somehow, thanks to their skills and training, they're flawless in their profession. They make it look simple as if what they do is easy. The rest of us may never realize how much hard work and how many sacrifices they may had to endure, how many times they had to wake up at four every morning and go to bed after 10 p.m. most days. No vacation time, their children barely know them, and in many sad situations, they are divorced by spouses who do not want to settle for this arduous life.

I am not advocating that people should throw family life, love, friendship, and the things that bring purpose to our life away to focus only on professional success, but I am simply saying that we sometimes forget or fail to realize that what we see is the final product. We sometimes forget the multiple steps in-between to reach that final product. What is even worse is that we often fail to realize that those multiple steps in-between could have been performed by any one of us to reach the same level of success.

This may be the biggest misconception of success. And it may be that not all of us are driven to succeed; that is okay. What is not okay is for you to ignore what is possible; in fact, it is actually impossible not to realize your heart's desires if you go after them with enthusiastic passion, create goals for your top five desires, take action every day toward their realization, have the courage to never give up, value your resources, invest in yourself, give back by way of investing in others, and create a legacy.

Even though too many times the toils of success may not be as beautiful as the final product, the hope of the *7 Checklist Items for Success* that you achieve the level of success you desire while, at the same time, keeping in focus what matters most in life (family, friendship, and a sense of making a difference in the lives of those around you) and savoring the sweet nectar and aroma of the flowers along the way. Whatever you do, please do not take the easy way—for the most difficult road is almost always the surest way to success and joy.

MOVING FORWARD: BE GRATEFUL FOR YOUR PAST

The fact that you have struggled in the past does not mean you will continue to struggle in the future, just like your past successes do not guarantee your future success. We can consider the present as the path linking our past to our future. Our daily actions are the steps we take on that path. Moving forward, what kind of steps will you be taking? Will they be steps of courage based on integrity? Will these steps be consistent with your goals? Will you be just going through the motions and wondering how you ended up shipwrecked and heartbroken in the distant future? For all of us, our present path linking our past to our future is full of uncertainties. We need to be courageous to walk it with the confidence that our tomorrow will be better than our yesterday.

Even though our past successes do not guarantee our future success, we need to understand that we should focus on what is perfect in our lives now, because whatever we focus on persists. Do not try to walk someone else's path just because it seems less arduous than yours. The outcome will only lead to dissatisfaction. You need to be courageous in following your passion and in pursuing your goals for the future.

Most people think that success is difficult, when in fact what is difficult is remaining consistent in pursuit of our daily goals and doing what we know we need to do each day toward the realization of our ultimate goals. For example, there is nothing positive that can come from watching television, yet most of us have a big-screen television set in our living room and very few books on success in our library. In fact, few of us have a library in our house at all.

We all know that the knowledge we need to achieve success can be found in self-help or autobiographies of successful people. You may not know that most successful people wake up by four o'clock in the morning to spend at least two hours focusing on their goals and planning their day. Very few of us who aren't yet successful do the same, even though we claim we want to be successful.

We all know that our biggest resource is time, and that the most successful people take full advantage of the 24 hours of their day. Yet most of us will waste time doing things like going to the bar, hanging out in night clubs, or surfing on social media. It is a no-brainer that wasted time is not useful for the success we claim we want. True success is not difficult; what is difficult is breaking our unproductive habits. Most people will resume their old habits even after reading these words. The question is, will you be one of those people? Or will you have the courage to make the hard choice and decide to take action to get control of your time, set goals, and take actions today toward a more successful life for tomorrow?

BE CONFIDENT ABOUT THE FUTURE

Just as we are confident when we leave our home each day that we will return home later, or just as we are confident when we say goodbye to our friends that we will see them again soon, we need to be as confident about the realization of our goals in the future.

At the risk of sounding contradictory, we should also have a sense of urgency in our life. For example, even though it does not cross our mind, there is always the possibility that somewhere and somehow someone may not be lucky enough to return home one day due to a misfortune, an accident, or a medical crisis. There is also the possibility that you may never see that family member or friend again you just said goodbye to. While it is important to be confident in the realization of your goals in the future, make sure to have that sense of urgency in the actions that you take and in your interaction with the people around you. Many people live their lives as if they were a feather being swept away in life's stormy wind. They don't plan or have goals for their future. You should be different and plan your day as if it were your last day on this earth.

Having a sense of urgency will also give you the necessary courage to move through each day toward the accomplishment of your goals. It will also stimulate you to live your life to the fullest by loving and cherishing not only the people who are in your circle, but also everyone else you meet. You will find yourself looking more into the eyes of your loved ones, and you will notice yourself appreciating people around you much more. You will show more gratitude to others, and you will certainly express your deepest emotions and become more adept at recognizing the emotions of those around you. They will come to understand that you truly care about them.

I hope reading this passage does not scare you, but instead helps you to understand how short life can be. While you may still have much to accomplish, remember to enjoy what you do and the people around you for who they are because they may not always be there, and you may not always be here. As you are working on the realization of your goals, don't forget to plan to visit that special place you have always wanted to visit, read that book you have always wanted to read, or learn that new hobby you have always wanted to enjoy. Be confident about your goals for the future and always have a sense of urgency in all that you do in the present.

THE COURAGE TO MAINTAIN A POSITIVE ATTITUDE

During the course of your life, you should strive to be in control of your attitude. People may act in ways that are not consistent with your values, their views of the outcome that you seek may differ, or you may not always be successful in obtaining the results you desire. Even so, there is one aspect of your life that you are in control of and should always remain in control of—your attitude.

Striving to maintain a positive mental attitude in all things will not always be possible. But before you can display a positive attitude in all that you do, you need to start by *having* a positive attitude. It all starts in the mind; change your mind, and you will change your life. Just like the forefathers of the United States demonstrated a positive mindset by focusing on making the newly formed union "more perfect" instead of focusing on improving its imperfections, you should also have the same outlook on life and focus on what is positive—on what is perfect and strive to make it more perfect. This is what positive mental attitude is.

It is possible that some people will argue that making something more perfect is the same as improving its imperfection; nothing can be further from the truth. When you say you will make something more perfect, you are focusing on the positive aspect of it. For example, if your mental attitude is to have more perfect success in your life, the images you are displaying to your brain are the images of your previous successes. These previous successes may vary (e.g., the A you earned in that difficult class, the job you were lucky enough to have, the promotion you received, your health, etc.). Vice versa, if you decide to focus on the imperfections in your life, the images you project to your brain are negative. The key thing to note is that whatever we focus on in our mind will persist in our life. Hence, have the courage and the discipline to always focus on the positive or the perfection aspect of your life and keep striving to make them more perfect and more positive each day.

WE DON'T GET TO BE SUCCESSFUL, WE BECOME SUCCESSFUL

Many people believe that becoming successful in life is difficult when in fact what is difficult is garnering the courage needed daily to fight the small battles one at time to make the right decisions or to take the right actions toward a successful life. No matter how small these battles may be, as long as you are moving toward the future that you want, you are winning. Always remember the small battles that you avoid today may become the wars of your tomorrow. We need to have the courage to always say the truth, even though at times telling a lie is more convenient. It takes courage to keep silent when we have nothing to say or to add to the conversation, it takes courage to speak up when our voice can make a difference and bring change to help improve the lives of others, and it takes courage to strive to maintain our integrity.

What many of us fail to have the courage to accept and what we many times fail to realize is that we don't get to be successful; we become successful. Success is not a gift that a parent can give to a child. It is something that the child him or herself will have to become. The confusion is that we sometimes associate wealth with success. It is true that successful people are wealthy—they cannot help it because wealth is a byproduct of success. But you don't become successful because you are wealthy; instead, we become wealthy because we are successful. Success is something we metamorphose into. The difference is that we control every step of the transformation through our goals, our actions, our courage, the value we place on our resources, our investment in ourselves and others, our commitment to giving back by improving the lives of others, and our legacy. You are truly in control of all these steps. The transformation will only start the moment you decide to believe that you and only you are indeed in control of your success in life and your destiny.

THE COURAGE TO SAY NO

In your quest for a more successful life, you will encounter multiple distractions and your attention will be pulled in many different directions. You will likely face the biggest challenge that most successful people face on a daily basis: time restriction. The solution is not easy; however, the beauty is that the solution is simple. In fact, it is only a two-letter word. This two-letter word is *no*.

Don't let this two-letter word fool you. It takes courage, indeed, a lot of courage to say no. It takes courage to say no to the people around you when they truly believe that you are the solution to their problem. It takes courage to say no to attending that birthday party. It takes courage to say no to accepting that other collateral duty. It takes courage to say no to going over your budget. It takes courage to say no to going to the bar with your friends. It takes courage to say no to letting that friend or that family member borrow another sum of money from you.

The good news is that while saying no will take a lot of courage initially, over time you will find it easier to make those decisions— as long as you are doing it for the right reason. By saying no, you let the other person know that you have your priorities straight. Even though you should always stand ready to help someone in need, you should never let yourself be manipulated to support someone's lifestyle when you know they should be making better choices themselves. Someone may be facing an unfortunate circumstance, and in that case by all means you should help him. You should trust that you will know when that need is real. While some people will not be happy with you saying no to them, over time they will come to respect you for standing up for yourself and to them for saying no. Despite the way that others may initially make you feel, you need to believe in the instinct and wisdom of all the successful people who rely on the power of this two-letter word and have learned to love it for its beauty.

If you have children, you are probably already an admirer of this beautiful, two-letter word. Go ahead and say it one more time: *no*. Again. No, no, *no*. What you will end up realizing is that by having the courage to say *no* to the things that will hinder you from achieving your goals, you are actually saying *yes* to the things and people that can help you achieve your goals.

THE COURAGE TO SAY YES

It is only fitting to end this chapter about courage on a positive note. I hope that by now you have realized that courage is an essential part of the seven checklist items for a more successful life. Make courage your tireless coach, the voice that will cheer you up when discouragements set in. That voice will push you to take one more step when you feel that you have nothing more to offer. Make courage the voice that reminds you that the sun is always about to come up after it is the darkest. Finally, make courage the voice that will reaffirm your intuition that yes, there *is* a more successful life awaiting you. Obtaining a more successful life will not be easy; however, this book is not about ease. You will need to strive and pay the price for a more successful life. Always be ready to do what it takes to achieve your goals.

Will you be tired at times? Yes. Will the prospect of giving up ever cross your mind? Yes. Will it be easier to just go through life without that feeling of going against the current? Yes. But have the courage to take actions that will move you forward toward your goals. Remember, as part of your quest to a more successful life, it is your obligation to value resources. You should not only value your resources, but also the resources around you—whether they are yours or not.

The next chapter will explain what valuing resources is all about. Let me first say that valuing resources involves knowing what your core competencies are (as well as those of other people). Valuing resources is not about hoarding what you have. It is not about taking all of the available resources. Valuing resources is not about conservation of resources because of your misperception of limitation. It is about bringing more value to your resources as well as the resources around you. It is about bringing hope and creating a better life for you and others.

CHAPTER 4
VALUE
RESOURCES

Your time is your most valued possession, but it is usually given away—wasted by the poor while cherished like a treasure by the rich. Always remember that human resources, starting with your own, are the greatest resources in the industry. Be genuinely interested and enthusiastic about everyone you meet. Learn about them and be sure to remember the name of everyone you meet. Always value yourself and adopt the appearance and the gravitas of a Chief Executive Officer. Others will judge you by your actions, your appearance, your character, and your communication. Dress in a way that anyone could pick you from a group and which characterizes you as the CEO among your peers. Remember to fake it until you make it.

YOU CANNOT APPRECIATE THE VALUE OF WHAT YOU DON'T KNOW

Be clear on your definition of assets. Think of assets as a generator of income and resources that can be converted into a greater sum than what you originally invested. Think like an entrepreneur. In his book *Rich Dad, Poor Dad*, Robert T. Kiyosaki helps you further understand what assets are, but for the purpose of this chapter we can consider assets to be wealth. That wealth may be financial, intellectual, or anything that you can make more valuable than you found it. You will notice that the people who generate the most assets in any organization tend to be those who are most passionate about what they do. To put it more simply, the assets generated by human resources are directly proportional to the passion that someone has for what they do.

If a janitor is passionate about being a janitor, she will have more motivation to learn to become the best janitor that there is, and as a result, she will be among the most valuable janitors in that particular enterprise. The same can be said about any profession, whether law, fast food, or medicine. The more passionate you are about your job, the more motivated you will be to study it. As a result, you will become better at it and will most likely generate more valuable returns or assets for that enterprise. You can bet that your boss will consider you a valuable asset, because you create more value for the company. The more value you create for the company or for the world, the more valuable you become.

Martin Luther King said it best during his speech on April 9, 1967: "If a man is called to be a street sweeper, he should sweep streets even as Michelangelo painted, Beethoven composed music, or Shakespeare wrote poetry. He should sweep streets so well that all the hosts of heaven and earth will pause to say, here lived a great street sweeper who did his job well." If you follow this advice from Dr. Martin Luther King, Jr., you will realize a simple fact of life missed by so many people: We are our own treasure in life. All we have to do is find out what we are passionate about, perfect it by being the best at it, and the rest will be history.

One of the first things to do if you value resources is to understand your core competency and the core competencies of the people around you. You may not be able to fully recognize what your core competencies are, and others will likely say the same. This challenge makes it much more difficult to determine what others' core competencies are. I will not attempt to downplay this dilemma. All I can say is, the more you consider this question (whether focusing on yourself or others), the more comfortable you will be arriving at the answers. It is impossible to find answers to questions we do not ask.

One way you may find the answers is by asking yourself the question a different way. Consider asking yourself instead what your purpose is in life. Or, why are you here? Why were you the one lucky enough to be born instead of the countless other individuals who could have been at the moment of your conception? What purpose do you serve in life? If there were one thing you could achieve in your lifetime that would convince you that your time on earth was spent well, what would it be? What is that one thing that, when you do it, makes you feel more alive, more passionate, and more content? Have you ever done something that seemed to make time stand still, and it feels like an out-of-body experience? What is that thing that you do that leaves you feeling more energized after you've already finished doing it? These answers may come immediately, or they may require some soul-searching. Nevertheless, once you can answer these questions with conviction, you've likely found your core competencies.

Once you find out what your core competencies are, your job is to make them your craft. Focus your attention on excelling in them, honing them, and becoming the very best that you can be at them. Your job is also to encourage others to do the same about their core competencies. The more people you help succeed in achieving their goals, the closer you will come to achieving your own goals. Success in life is not a zero-sum game; it is indeed a win-win situation.

If this concept sounds contrary to what you've previously been taught, that's probably because you have not spent enough time with successful people. The more time you spend with successful people, the more you will realize how open they are to helping others to become successful in life. If you still have some doubt, think about the autobiographies of the successful men and women of this world. If they did not want to help others to be successful, why do you think by the time they reached the summit of their life's success, and before they departed this world, out of all the things that they could have done with their time, they decided to write an autobiography that recounts their life's journey and the steps to their success?

Don't let your perception of non-successful people cloud your judgment of successful people. The actions of successful people are contrary to the "crabs in the bucket" analogy (the crabs in the bucket keep pulling on each other's legs, dragging them down). Successful people want to pull others up to a more successful, healthy, and wealthy life. They want to tell you that there are plenty of places for you at the summit and that the view is beautiful. They want to pull you up to be the best you that you can be: the best father, the best mother, the best daughter, the best son, the best wife, or the best husband. Successful people want to add, contribute, and invest in you by increasing your value. They are the experts at valuing resources; they like to create and build. If you want to join them, continue reading.

VALUING RESOURCES NOW

People often erroneously convince themselves that they will start valuing their resources when they have more. For example, they say that they would go to the gym if they had more time or they would take better care of their car if they had the car of their dreams. The misconception is that they never feel like they have enough because they focus only on the end goals without considering the smaller daily actions needed to achieve them. A couple was living in a rented one-bedroom apartment and said they'll start valuing and managing their resources when they buy a house. After they buy that house, they'll then move that end goal to when they pay off that house or when their kids go to college. The example above is commonplace today and can be replaced with a myriad of other excuses.

They should start by valuing what they have now while they are living in that one-bedroom apartment, and their goals should be focused on bringing more value to their current resources, no matter how small or limited they may be. After all, what may be one person's limited resources may be someone else's abundance. If you don't believe that your limited resources may be someone else's treasure, take a trip to some of the poorest countries in the world or watch a few videos on YouTube about them. No matter how bad you believe your situation may be, someone else is going through worse.

The truth is that you are not helping yourself or your situation by focusing on your lack of better resources. You will always feel better by focusing on the good in that moment. You have a roof over your head while someone else is sleeping in the rain; you have a car while someone else is walking or riding public transportation an hour or more to get work, etc. While your resources may seem to be limited relative to the resources you choose to compare them to, the secret to a more successful life is to value what you have now. Don't wait until you have more. Be grateful in the moment for that moment.

VALUABLE RESOURCES SHOULD ALWAYS BE VIEWED AS ASSETS

On your road to a more successful life, one of the reasons to value your resources is that resources are assets. Once you know what your core competencies are, it is easier to transform them into assets. By viewing valuable resources as assets, you will view the time you spend on realizing your goals as chips that you can collect upon achieving your success in life. By valuing resources as assets, you will use your time more consciously, and each moment and each hour of your time will be more useful and valuable to you. You will also get to appreciate and value the time of other people more. By valuing your time and other people's time as assets, your interactions and your actions will not only leave you and others better off than you started, but they will also make your life better than before with each interaction. By making your life and the lives of other people better each time, you can be sure you are indeed making the world a better and more valuable place thanks to your actions.

Please remember, you must truly view the interests of others like your own. Treat people with respect and integrity, just like you want to be treated. Never seek to cheat others, as you are only cheating yourself out of your morals and compromising your integrity in the process. The principles explained in this book are about making you understand that valuable resources can be created by building more value in each other. Always seek and strive to increase value especially in places where others don't. Perhaps it is a property in need of repair, an affordable used car, the purchase of some undervalued stocks, the purchase of a small business, or faster ways to get a job done. Develop the reputation of a person who creates value in resources.

Success is the realization of your life's ideal, the realization of whatever gives you the deepest joy and satisfaction. Success is doing something that you would have done anyway hour after hour, day after day, year after year, even if you weren't paid for it. Money is just a gauge of the value you provide to others and society. The more valuable the service you provide to others, the more money you will be paid in return to for that service. Hence, the better you are at whatever you do, the more money you're likely to earn. It is just that simple. Money is just compensation you receive for the service you render to others and society. Following the checklist for a more successful life or success in general is about pursuing your real passion, your ideal goals, and a flourishing life. The money will always follow. What you choose to do with that money is up to you to decide.

BE HUMBLE IN VICTORY

As you learn to value the resources around you, other people who might not fully understand your goals for a more successful life may view your attempts at creating value as materialistic simply from ignorance (or arrogance). For you, valuing resources may just be a reflection of your gratitude from a sense of satisfaction of having the resources in the first place. Perhaps, it may also be a sense of pride from a joyful victory lap. In such a dilemma, I recommend you heed the advice of former U.S. President, George W. Bush, "Be humble in victory." While I encourage you to value the resources around you, you should do so in humility and grace. You need to accept people the way they are during that particular moment in their life while seeking to encourage them to follow their passions and their core competencies.

It may be helpful to remember that it is difficult for people to change. The habits of the past are difficult to break. But if you show signs of humility, people may be more inclined to help you bring more value to your resources and be more willing to accept the simple fact that your honest intention is simply to help them bring value to their resources as well. The reality is the more someone has been taken advantage of in the past, the more likely they will question your desires and your actions of bringing value to their resources. Once people realize your sincerity, they will follow you like a flood and they will be willing to help create a new path to a more successful life.

During your quest for a more successful life, are you creating value and success for both yourself *and* others? If the answer is yes to such a question, trust that others will also eventually see and accept this truth. During your quest of creating more value, you should avoid giving others even the slightest impression of superiority, as if you want to be better than everyone else and seek to walk a path different from the pack. In doing so, you will likely cause them to resist helping you achieve your goals.

You need to be transparent about your true desires of simply wanting to find answers to your own questions in life. You need to help them understand that your desire is to help them achieve their own successes and that helping them is just part of your quest to find and develop your own potential. Let them understand that this is a win-win situation where all can become better in the process. That your purpose is not to take advantage of anyone else, just like your purpose is not to let others succeed at your own detriment. Instead, your intent is to create an environment where all can flourish. Many choose not to believe in such a noble objective, and you should not blame them—after all, they have grown to see others display exactly the opposite behavior all around them. As actions speak louder than words, I hope that your actions and humility will show through and help them to understand that not only are your objectives possible, but they should be the new way of conducting business.

Be prepared for the critic to call you naïve but let the result of your accomplishments of a more successful life be your advocate. It is possible to show humility in the midst of your victories and doing so will only help others achieve more victories. Why, you may ask? This is because when you show humility in your victories, you encourage others to show the same grace and humility through their struggles which increases *their* success. For that, they will always be grateful to you because they have seen how other winners have treated their adversaries in the past. Learning to put yourself in someone's else shoes is learning to have empathy toward them, which helps you to show more humility toward them.

Please be aware that at first this will feel strange to you and will look strange to others, but there is no other more efficient way to get others to support you without coercion or deceit as the lives of the great leaders in the world have shown us. It is possible to show confidence in your goals and create valuable resources while at the same time remaining humble. This is possible when the result that you are seeking transcends your own selfish reasons. The increased value you are seeking to add to the resources around you is not just for you, but for the betterment of others through the opportunities that you will create. The humility and conviction that leaders like Abraham Lincoln, Martin Luther King, Mother Theresa, Muhammad Yunus, and many others of the past and present have displayed go beyond their own accomplishments. By displaying humility even in your proudest victories, you, too, can have an ever-lasting impact on the lives of those around you.

VALUE PEOPLE AND TIME; THEY'RE BOTH FLEETING

Valuing resources is about focusing on what is the most important in your life and the lives of people around you. Your past experiences have likely revealed two realities of life: People and time are the most valuable resources because both are fleeting. It is important to realize that people have different interests and different core competencies. Just like you would not place a truck tire on a sedan car or vice versa, you would ensure the right people be chosen for the right task. While you think it would not be too useful to ask a carpenter to give you surgical advice or to ask a surgeon to give you carpentry advice, it is quite strange to think how frequently we fail to seek advice from the right person or hire the right person for the job.

Time is one of your most valuable resources. Once this second, this minute, this hour, this day, this week, this month, or this year passes, you will never get it back. We are all aware of the passing aspect of time, yet we seldom show a sense of urgency and sense that each moment matters—the feeling that if something needs to be done, it should be done now. The strange thing is that most of us, no matter our age, tend to believe we have time until we run out of time. We fail to understand that whether we take action or not, life will go on. Most of us know a person whom we believed had all the time ahead of him or her who has ended up passing away. If you keep it in your heart that people and time are your most valuable resources, you will always be able to see them for the treasure that they are, and you will undoubtedly make them your most precious assets. When it comes to people and time, are your actions contributing to your betterment and the betterment of those around you? If the answer is not a resounding *yes*, please reconsider your goals.

Again, never fool yourself by trying to take advantage of other people. By working to increase your valuable resources and those of other people, your actions combined with theirs will create cooperation. If your intention is to take advantage of people, however, you will certainly destroy your own valuable resource; this is just how life works. If you try to deceive others, sooner or later it will catch up to you. It just isn't worth it.

If you live your life by always doing your best and striving to give more than you have received, then another simple fact is that the wisdom of life will be yours to keep in treasure bags. This wisdom is that, in life, you will realize that living a more successful life is not about how much you can get from others but rather how much you can give to others. Let's state it again: *Life is not about how much you can get from others, but about how much you can give to others.* Also, never allow yourself to forget that everybody has a story, a story that is, in fact, the base of their core identity.

In your quest to value resources for a more successful life, you need to know, listen to, understand, and show empathy to the stories of the people around you. You need to understand that people's resources can only be discovered by listening to their stories. Remember that everybody has a story. Listen to them and learn to appreciate them for who they are. You probably will be the most valuable to them and they likely will be the most valuable to you after you know their story. Use the adage that we have two ears and one mouth, so we can listen more than we speak.

Ask them about their stories, themselves, their families, and about their passions. Always make sure that the other person speaks more during every conversation. Each time you meet a new person, at the end of the conversation, can you say that you truly know their story? If not, did you arrange to meet with them again to learn more about them?

You may think that it is impractical to learn the story of everyone that you meet. To that, I will answer, if it is worth it to meet new people, it is worth it to know their stories. Remember, as humans, we tend to do things for others that we wouldn't do for ourselves. If it is worth doing, it is worth doing right because whatever you are doing, you are doing it for someone else because you care. Hence, remember it is not about you, but the other person. Also, remember that both that other person and time are fleeting; therefore, waste no time to act with urgency and show them how much that you value them both.

BE CONSISTENT IN HOW YOU VALUE RESOURCES

Be consistent in how you value all your resources. If you say you believe that people and time are the world's most valuable resources, yet you don't respect and show appreciation to the people around you, are routinely late, or generally waste time and fail to take care of yourself physically, mentally, or spiritually, what does that say about your consistency? The point here is, while you should normally value these characteristics as the yardstick with which you value resources, you should always make sure that the person you see in the mirror also has these characteristics.

If you said you believe that time is a valuable resource, but you are always late and always waste time in unfruitful activities, what does it profit you? These actions are obviously not consistent with your reported belief. Be clean, be precise, be organized, and always keep your resources in their optimal condition. At risk of repetition, remember that resources are meant to bring more resources into your life that will increase in value. Your values and resources are assets; learn to take care of what you have.

I stated earlier that people and time are the most valuable resources. The question is, how are you managing these resources? Do you keep yourself clean, both physically and mentally? Do you always make sure that your clothes are clean and that your appearance reflects that of a Fortune 500 CEO? Does the information that you put in your mind by reading, listening, or thinking positively contribute to your desires to a more successful life? Are the foods that you eat healthy for your body? Do you exercise routinely? Do you use your time wisely? Do you have a schedule and a to-do list?

If the answer to any single one of the above questions is not a resounding *yes*, ask yourself why not. Can you commit yourself to doing something about it right now? Do not procrastinate, remember time is fleeting and if an action needs to be taken, the decision needs to be made right now. One of the surest ways for people not to trust you is if they notice that your actions are not consistent with what you say, your stated priorities or your professed values. You need to make sure that you are consistent with everything that you say. Even the people who are the closest to you, who love you the most, and who are your biggest fans will question your integrity if you are not consistent.

How do you become a consistent person, you may ask? The answer is simple, do the right thing. Do the things that you know you need to do to get you to the realization of your goals, even though these things are difficult and no one else is watching. Being consistent is waking up two hours earlier than you have to every morning, having a to-do list every morning, and having a schedule that details the actions you need to take during the course of your day. Being consistent is to tirelessly seek to increase the value of your resources and the value of the resources of the people around you. Being consistent is to effectively use every moment of each day toward the accomplishment of your goals, even if you don't feel like it.

If you have trouble taking action, just follow the 5 Second Rule of Mel Robbins without thinking twice. Just do it! For those of you reading this book who may have a family, you will be surprised that the people around you, especially kids, learn more from watching what you do than by listening to what you say. Instead of talking about excellence, do the acts of excellence each day and there will be no need to ask them to do the same because they will follow you on their own.

If you are a leader, do the things that you want your followers to do. If the business leader cares about employees, the employees will care for the business. There is wisdom in the words of Luke 6:31

from the Bible, "Do unto others as you would have them do unto you." Humans are social beings, they mimic the actions of others around them. You should strive to be the leader that they can follow; the pathfinder of the trail you want them to navigate. The road to a more successful life is difficult and at times will be lonely, but the fruit of a more successful life is so much sweeter when enjoyed with others. Help as many people as are willing to be as successful or even more successful than you. There is a synergy and additive effect in helping others and you can indeed give more than you have received as long as you remain consistent with the way you value resources.

HAVE A BUDGET

In this book, very few things mentioned have been about money. Contrary to what most people believe, money is a result of success, not the cause of success. If money is what you want in life, you may be relieved to learn that the key to financial freedom is to first start by creating income via entrepreneurship (own a patent, create a business, create a product, or create whatever it is that people need). The limitation in creating income, as you have learned earlier, is time since you only have 24 hours a day.

This brings us to the second key to generate wealth, and that is to invest. Once you earn your income through entrepreneurship, you can invest that income in rental properties, or be a money lender. Again, if money is the only thing you are seeking, the following three books do greater justice to this subject: *Rich Dad, Poor Dad* by Robert T. Kiyosaki, *Money Master the Game* by Tony Robbins, or *The Millionaire Fastlane* by MJ DeMarco.

Returning to our topic, having a budget will help you avoid or at least limit the stress of money in your life. Having a budget is like having a daily schedule: You have to keep it on track. The key is to make a budget by the first of the month and strive to follow it throughout the month. The reason why having a budget at this point is important is because if you can stay on budget while you have little, you will be able to stay on budget when you have more than enough. The other benefit of staying on budget is that no matter how much money you make, it can always be spent at a faster rate than it took to accumulate it.

The ability to spend money at a faster rate than you can accumulate it is true for anyone, no matter his profession. For example, a lawyer may easily spend the $15,000 yearly salary of a farmworker in one day. Now, the farmworker may consider that impossible, but this is entirely possible for the lawyer. If that lawyer doesn't have a budget and continues to spend like this routinely, one can understand that very soon, she may face financial ruin. While the farmworker who stays on a budget may continue to maintain his lifestyle, support his family abroad, and at the same time put 10% of his salary aside for savings.

Not having a budget is likely the biggest contributing factor of people being two to three paychecks away from financial ruin. It's is why most people force themselves to go to their job, even though they are sick or have a sick family member at home. Having a budget will provide you with the savings you need to invest in your future. It will provide you with the down payment that you need to put down on your house, or the funds to buy your house in full.

Learning to stay on budget each month is not easy. If it were, everybody would have done it by now. Also remember, this book is not about easy; rather, it is about taking action and going through the checklist of a more successful life. If you happen to be having difficulty planning a budget or staying on budget each month, you may greatly benefit from reading *The Richest Man in Babylon* by George S. Clason and *The Total Money Makeover: A Proven Plan for Financial Fitness* by Dave Ramsey or going to one of his seminars about financial success. I found both of these men very informative.

KNOW WHAT YOU DON'T KNOW AND LISTEN TO OTHERS

As you start to value resources around you, you will reaffirm, or in some cases realize, that you don't know everything. What is important is that by valuing resources around you, you will know where to find the answers. You likely know some people who know the answer to your question, so in that case, seek their advice and listen to them if it makes sense. In a situation where no one you know has the answer, ask if they know someone else who can provide you with that answer.

While it is always a good idea to ask advice from the foremost expert, in the case you don't have access to the very best expert, you may have to ask for a second or third opinion. In general, most people tend to not like your asking someone else's opinion after they gave you theirs. My advice is you should always thank them and explain to them that you had planned to solicit the advice of other people as well because you want to appreciate all the nuances of the situation.

Even though it is rare, once in a while an expert is wrong. It is important that after you receive a satisfactory answer to your question, you act on it as soon as possible. The only thing worse than asking the same question to more than one expert is not acting on the advice given. There is no excuse for it! You will only be wasting your time and the time of those around you. The more comfortable you become at valuing resources, the more comfortable you will be at accepting the advice of the expert you know and trust.

THE SECRET TO MORE VALUABLE RESOURCES

Earlier in this chapter, you were introduced to the idea that time and people are the most valuable resources. In this section, you will learn a key distinction that helps you distinguish the most valuable people around you. The question you are probably asking yourself is how do you find the right people? Let's start with this quote from Zig Ziglar: "Your attitude, not your aptitude, will determine your altitude in life." What kind of attitude was Zig referring to? If you guessed a positive attitude, you are correct. What Zig is saying is that how far you will reach in life does not depend on how smart you think you are or how smart your parents or others think you are, but your level of success will be directly correlated to your attitude.

When you start observing people to determine their core competencies and value as a resource, you should start by focusing on their attitude. Someone with a positive attitude will display energy and enthusiasm from the outset, before you even start talking to them. You may even be able to guess people's energy by just observing them passing by at the park. Once you start talking with them, you can confirm whether your assumption of their energy was correct or not. My assumption is you will be right most of the time by observing their energy level or their level of enthusiasm.

Why is a positive mental attitude so important? This is an important question, but one that is difficult to explain. It is like oxygen: You may not be able to fully explain it or see it, but you know that it is there. We can define a positive mental attitude as having an optimistic outlook on life. Such an outlook is important if you believe the outcome of your life in the next five years is an accumulation of your mental attitude and what you are focused on most of the time.

Think back five years ago. You may be surprised to realize that your current life is just a reflection of the things you were thinking about 5 or 10 years ago. Are you surprised at such a discovery? You are truly in control of changing your life's outcome by changing your current mental attitude to a more positive one. More importantly, you can vastly increase your valuable resources by surrounding yourself with people who have a positive mental attitude. If you choose to adhere to a more positive mental attitude, you will be an even more valuable resource to the people around you, and they will acknowledge that.

It is good advice to apply the following quote by Earl Nightingale more in our life. He states, "We become what we think about most of the time, and that is the strangest secret." Indeed, the secret to a more successful life is to create more valuable resources in your life by surrounding yourself with competent people who have a positive mental attitude. Just like the importance of oxygen in our life, some things in life that we truly need are the hardest to understand.

I hope you decide to take the leap of faith and decide to join the vast list of successful people who adopt a positive mental attitude as their way of life. Now that you know the secret to creating more valuable resources to lead to a more successful life is through a positive mental attitude, I would like you to reflect for a moment on what you have learned thus far in the 7 *Checklist Items for Success*.

In the first chapter, you learned the importance of writing the five goals that reflect the purpose of your life and that you want to accomplish the most. In chapter 2, you learned the importance of taking actions by devoting the first two hours of your day toward the realization of your five goals. In chapter 3, you learned the importance of courage to commit to taking daily actions toward the realizations of your five goals. In chapter 4, you learned about creating valuable resources toward your quest for a more successful life, based on the realization your five goals. Now you are about to start chapter 5, which will talk about investment. As you may have guessed, the purpose of investment is to create even more value to the previously obtained resources. This investment will have the potential to snowball the realization of a more successful life. Please continue reading.

INVESTING IN YOURSELF AND OTHERS

The most efficient way to invest in yourself is through hard work. Always invest in yourself in terms of learning about your profession. Seek to create value in yourself and in everyone around you. Always consider hard work to be the deposit to your account of success. While criticisms may act as unauthorized withdrawals from your success account, they can be converted to assets if you learn from them. Don't be cheated by them; instead, accept them objectively and learn to use them toward your growth.

NO BETTER RETURN THAN INVESTING IN YOURSELF AND MANAGING YOUR TIME

In chapter 4, you learned that people and time are by far the two most valuable resources. At my core, I believe that the satisfaction that comes from investing in yourself and others is the most rewarding and profitable return on your investment there could be. This is obvious in some instances, but not in others. You will be hard pressed to find a better investment prospect than an individual who believes in herself and decides to commit to self-improvement. Self-improvement can turn a poor person into a philanthropist, an uneducated person into a scholar, a vagabond into an officer, and a student into a professor. Any circumstance can be turned around into a more positive one by self-improvement. Indeed, in addition to a focus on self-improvement, you also seek to focus on the improvement of the people around you.

Aside from investing in yourself, to illustrate how important investing in another person can be, consider the following example of a child who grew up in poverty with nothing except the desire of one day becoming a lawyer to help improve not only her circumstance, but also the circumstances of those around her:

This child kept that desire throughout the years, and in high school happened to meet a teacher who believed in her dream and decided to give her a book written by a famous lawyer. Our young high school student was so moved by this book that she decided to continue reading books about this successful lawyer. She finds in those books the mentors and advisors she had always wanted. A few years later she was going to college and eventually became a lawyer.

By every account, we can agree that the time the teacher invested in this young woman could not have been a better investment. In this context, you can see the time investment of the teacher in that student was a great investment. Similarly, you should also consider your time as one of your two most important investments to your self-improvement. Invest every moment of your time to the realization of your goals and also to help those around you achieve their full potential. Yet this is not all there is to consider about investment. Even though there is more to the concept of investment in the usual sense of the word, time and people should be considered the base of investment for anyone who wants a more successful life. There are plenty of professionals whose sole expertise is to help you pick a financial investment consistent with your financial goals.

The purpose of this book is obviously not to be a replacement for the advice of professionals but is instead to reaffirm their importance and to show you some qualities of successful people that allow them to have the financial wealth to invest in the more traditional sense. Aside from investing in yourself, the people around you, and valuing each moment of your time, save at least 10% of everything you earn. Just like there is no better return on investment than investing in yourself and managing your time, there is no better use of your paycheck than paying off your debts.

GOOD INVESTMENTS FOR GOD ARE GOOD INVESTMENTS FOR YOU

When I was eight years old, due to unrest in Port-au-Prince, Haiti's capital, my mother sent me to live with my godmother in an area called Mirebalais. My godmother would take me to Mass every Sunday morning. Before the offering, the priest would explain that, as God's children, God expects us to give 10% of what we earn to him. The problem, though, was that the entire church community was poor. I felt that my godmother, a widower, was the poorest of them all. What shocked me was that she would give money in offering every Sunday, even though she was poor. How she had the courage to do that, I was not sure; all I kept thinking at that time was that she could have at least used that money to buy some meat for the next meal or save it to one day repair that old, dilapidated house of hers.

Needless to say, I couldn't dare to tell her what I was thinking for fear of getting smacked. In my mind, I kept hoping that at least one day the collection money would be given to her... or at least to me. I believed that such big amount of money, maybe the adjusted equivalent of $20-$100 USD per offering (which at that time represented a huge sum of money to me), would undoubtedly raise me out of poverty. I soon realized that the 10% of God's money from the cathedral was not going to be given to me or my godmother.

Somehow, when I grew up and started earning some income, I concluded from that experience that if 10% of all of our income is good enough to advance the teaching of a prosperous God, it should certainly also be good enough advice for me to follow to raise myself from poverty to wealth. I am a firm believer that, at the very least, it is important that you save at least 10% of your income, no matter how small you think your income is. You may believe that it is not enough to meet all your responsibilities and debt, but even at this stage when you may not be able to see all the benefits, you still need to have the courage and financial discipline to put this 10% aside. You'll see the reasons later on.

The 10% that you save should be invested in creating more resources. Your goal is to seek to increase your savings and keep adding to that 10% you set aside from your income. You want to come to the point where you can be saving at least 90% of your total income until your investments start generating returns that can support your lifestyle. Until such a time, your goal is to get to that point where you can live on only 10% of your income—this means that you can reinvest the other 90% of your income until you are able to live comfortably on the return from your investments.

Once you are able to live comfortably on the return earned from your investments, you will have the financial freedom to do the things that you enjoy the most in life, whether traveling or making a difference in the lives of others. The sky's the limit; you decide what you are passionate enough about and want to spend your time doing. And if the way you want to spend your time is to be at work because you love what you do, then continue working at your current job because you like it. The point is that you are in control.

I believe this may also be the right time to state something that may already be obvious to you: We were born in this world with only the gift of life and nothing else. Somehow *you* have made it, and you are now reading this book. You are even luckier than most. Many people do not even know how to read. The other obvious thing in life, which we often choose to ignore, is the fact that when we depart this world, we will not take any possessions with us, not even a breath of air. Even though we cannot take anything with us, however, your legacy will live on. You can leave something behind (more on that later).

Don't invest for selfish reasons. Life is really more than that; we are not here as characters in a big selfish play. I believe you are reading this book because you also feel the same way. You feel you have more in view, you feel you have something to give, something to contribute, and you feel that life can and should be better for so many others who are unlucky enough to be born into poverty, a harsh environment, or the wrong family. You are reading this book because you feel, deep inside, that you may be able to do something about how the play ends, even though we may never know for sure. Maybe it might be to save the life of a mother of eight children whose child has put these words on this page for you.

The purpose of a true investment is to create value that improves your life and the lives of others. Never invest with the mindset of hoarding wealth away from the people around you, but instead invest with the sincere desire and conviction of making the world a better place. Also, never limit yourself from thinking big in terms of the return possibilities. Have a positive attitude, be hopeful, be thoughtful, be smart, always think in terms of solving needs, and focus on the ultimate return on your investment. For example, if you save $2,000 and then invest it in a well-planned business opportunity designed to solve a need that many people have. If, after one year, that business opportunity solves the need of 6,000 people with a net gain of $1 for each person helped, you have just made an income of $4,000 on your investment. You can reinvest your portion of the profit back to the business as the owner as many times as you want.

By every definition, you are creating more value. If God asks that 10% of all that you earn should be given to his church (which for me means his people), that is a good investment for God and it should also be a good investment for you. Just like you arrived here with nothing, you will leave with nothing. We can still live with the knowledge that we are making a difference in the lives of those around us by investing in solving as many needs as possible.

EXAMPLE OF A TYPICAL INVESTMENT WITH EXTRAORDINARY RETURN

Now, let's think for a moment that you have just met a dishwasher working at a local restaurant making less than $15,000 a year. Let's say that you are the local clinic nurse who happens to meet this dishwasher, take a positive action, and invest in him. You decide to meet with this dishwasher once a month for a year. During each visit, your goals were to help determine his true desires and teach him the importance of writing down his five most important goals and taking action on them. You believe if he is able to realize them, it will change the outcome of his life positively.

Fast forward 10 years later. This dishwasher has now graduated from law school and is earning $200,000 as a junior partner of a law firm. Would you say this was a great investment of your 52 hours mentoring this dishwasher? Do you think your investment in developing his core competencies and giving him the opportunity to lead a more successful life was worth it? I hope you will say yes as this was indeed a great return on a very small investment. Because you gave him the courage to commit to his goals, he realized a more successful life.

How about the return on the investment for you? I am sure you would agree that such an investment is worth more than any financial or monetary value you could have gained from the 52 hours you committed to helping this dishwasher. But it gets even better. What if this dishwasher became a lawyer and retired from his law firm after 20 years and then decided to create a non-profit organization to help others achieve their highest potential? Through that work, you could positively affect the lives of millions.

I will ask you the same question from above one last time: How about the return on investment for you, the person who has mentored this dishwasher? Wouldn't you agree this is a great return on your investment in him? These types of investments are all around us. You can find them at church, restaurants, jails, the peace corps, on missionary trips in poor countries, or nearly everywhere else if you choose to focus on creating value in people's lives.

INVESTING IN PEOPLE WHO HAVE WHAT IT TAKES

What you will realize is that, in the truest spirit of investing, successful people are willing to invest in the people who they believe have what it takes to succeed. Successful people are typically great judges of character. Yet successful people know how difficult the journey to a more successful life can be. It is not the purpose of this book to decide whom successful people should choose to support or to debate whether this is right or wrong. You can use this knowledge to propel yourself to success knowing that the more successful you are, the more successful others around you will become. This is because not only will you gain more confidence toward the realization of your goals, but other people will notice what hard work can bring about and they will imitate you. What you should not do, however, is wait there on the road to success for somebody to come mentor you.

The question is, then, how do you acquire what it takes to be successful? Answer this question from the point of view of a successful person. On average, most successful people say that there are three crucial ingredients to success:

1. **Goals.** Successful people believe that to become successful, one has to have goals to look forward to—an incentive, in other words. Once you reach your goals, you should immediately create new ones. This is important because after you have reached all your goals, if you don't set new goals, you will feel quite dissatisfied, empty, and desirous for something more. The solution is to have goals that require continuous improvements. You should seek

to create goals that never stop giving you returns on your investments.

2. **A mentor.** Your mentor could be God or a leader whose success you want to reflect upon during your realization of a more successful life. Successful people believe that they should strive to learn about other successful people by reading their books and studying any other material they may have. This is important because in our quest for success, we are initially surrounded by people who may not really want to achieve their full potential. Looking up to successful people and reading about them will allow you to glimpse into the window of their life and reaffirm that yes, there *is* a possibility for a more successful tomorrow.

3. **Courage.** Your values, your energy, and your integrity to continuously improve yourself in everything you do and everyone around you will give you the courage to remain committed.

While you may think that these three points are too simplistic, you will be amazed to learn that countless successful people from Matthew McConaughey to Coach Lou Holtz have advised the same. When we peel away all the insignificant layers of life, we are left only with the most important bare necessities, which are nothing more than what we have done for other people to make their lives better. If you seek to always gain recognition, you will probably end up feeling small and inferior. If you were to strive each day to invest in other people, however, you would certainly live a life of significance.

It does not matter how much has been given to you; what matters is how much you have given to others. Don't dwell on the fact that some people don't love you; what matters is how much you love others. Remember that we only have 24 hours a day, and the needs around us are many. You should never stop investing in people who have the desire for a more successful life. Therefore, direct anyone who desires a more successful life to follow the seven checklist items presented in this book. When you seek to invest in other people, you shouldn't seek perfection, because the truth is that none of us are perfect. The key, however, is to seek to invest in people who desire and strive to be a little more perfect each day.

THE POWER OF INVESTMENT

Investing in oneself is the only force powerful enough to transform someone from a struggling individual to a more successful person. The only force strong enough to transform a dishwasher to a physician, a cab driver to a lawyer, or the son of a single mother to a president is the *power of investment*. Investing in oneself is the only force strong enough to undo the belittling words of an oppressive authority figure to its subjects. Investing in oneself is the only force strong enough to raise the slave and the oppressed to freedom.

You don't have to look far to realize the marvelous feats of success that can be accomplished by investing in oneself. Start with the story of some of the people around you or look back in the history books at the story of Abraham Lincoln. Yet, very few people want to make the time investment of waking at up at four o'clock each morning to work toward a goal. They complain it is too early, too hard, or they are too tired. The truth is, they refuse to wake up four o'clock each morning because they don't have an important enough reason to. If your *why* is to prevent your children from dying of hunger in front of you, you will wake up at four o'clock. If your *why* is to wake up early to care for a sick spouse or child before you go to work, you will do it. As a human, our *why* is often to care for the people we love and is bigger than our own *why*. It is why you will see a single mother working two jobs so her sons and daughters never have to go through the life of struggle and need like she did. This is why a father or mother wakes up to go to work to provide for his or her family. The point is if you have someone you care enough for, your *why* will always be big enough to wake up at 4 a.m. to work on your goals.

Look around you. Don't you have a least one person you value enough to wake up at four o'clock for? If you look deep enough into the people around you and take the time to listen to their stories, your *why* might just be big enough for you to commit to waking up at four o'clock every morning. If you look at some of the struggles people in your family, your community, your country, and around the world are going through, your *why* might just be big enough to wake at four o'clock and invest two hours in your life every day. At the end of the day, the question is not why you are doing it, but who you are doing it for?

INVESTMENT IS THE VEHICLE TO A MORE SUCCESSFUL LIFE

There are many things that will distract you from investing. None of these should be peer pressure, lack of financial knowledge, or a mindset of neediness. Such behaviors are not consistent with successful investors. Many people will try to maintain a lifestyle to keep up with their peers or to keep up with the expectations of how they believe people expect them to live based on their status or profession. While meeting such expectations may seem to be the norm, you don't have to fall for that. You need to remain consistent with your goals. I doubt that "keeping up with the Joneses" is part of your top five goals. Be consistent and keep your eye on what matters to your future instead of what matters to your present.

Instead of trying to keep up with your peers, your first stop on your path to a more successful life is paying off your debts and becoming debt-free as soon as possible. You need to think of debts as the enemy of investing. As part of your monthly budget, allocate as much (at least 10%) of your income as you can toward repaying your debts. This may seem impossible based on your current situation, but it is important that you take that first step in investing in a more successful future. It may require that you let go of some leisure spending you are currently doing. It might require that you sell some of the things that you have which may be considered liabilities. Maybe it's a boat that you rarely use, jewelry, a nice car, etc. Once you are debt-free, you need to make the commitment and have the courage to remain consistent with that commitment of *staying* debt free.

From an investment point of view, you always have to keep it simple. When you talk about assets, always think of assets as those things that bring in more money. Maybe it's the extra money that you earn from reselling items online each month, that extra income that you make from selling crafts or art, or that extra money that you will earn from getting another job. All of these examples are additional sources of income that you can create to help you pay off your debt.

Avoiding peer pressure and paying off your debt should be your priority; however, staying debt free in a society where you are under constant pressure to buy what you cannot afford is not an easy task. If you make the decision to only spend your money on the things which can create additional income (assets) versus buying things that will cost you money in the future (liabilities), you will be able to make the right decisions, and your path toward a more successful life will be clearer.

LACK OF FINANCIAL KNOWLEDGE LEADS TO MISCONCEPTIONS ABOUT INVESTMENT

Another misconception about investing, many would argue, is a lack of financial knowledge. Some people will argue that they shouldn't invest at the moment because they don't know what to invest in. This is unfortunate because it seems that those people don't view themselves and their time as their biggest asset. The key to investing is to start by investing in yourself. A good place to start investing in yourself is taking the Dale Carnegie Public Speaking Course or something similar offered in your area. This course is one of the most important you can take in your pursuit of a more successful life.

This is important because, as your most important asset, you will be called upon on more than one occasion to share your point of view or to explain your position to others. Your audience may range from your children and your spouse all the way to the CEO of your corporation. A trained public speaker will instantly grab the ear of listening individuals and will give you their trust. Invest in yourself by reading books by successful individuals. You may want to start with their autobiographies that will give you the best perspective. Self-improvement books are also good books to read monthly as part of your investment in yourself (good job for already doing that!).

Knowledge is acquired from long hours of dedicated studies. Knowledge takes effort, and you have to be consistent in order to acquire it. If a piece of knowledge is told once without anything to correlate it to, it will likely be lost in short-term memory. But if you constantly absorb and apply that knowledge, the neural links to that knowledge become more prominent, allowing you to access it easier.

Another piece of financial knowledge that many people fail to understand is the importance of time. As we have explained before, we only have 24 hours in a day, rich and poor alike. How do so many successful people accomplish so much in those 24 hours while others seem just to let their 24 hours pass them by each day? Learning to invest your time more wisely is an important part of financial literacy. Spend your time doing things that you can later convert into more valuable assets; at first, that will likely be reading. Successful people are avid readers because they realize more knowledge can be gained from reading books than any other use of their time.

My advice is to join a book club. Your reading will likely lead you to two decisions when it comes to investing in your financial resources. These two decisions are either feeling confident about investing in things that you believe in and knowing that you have a core competitive advantage or deciding to leave your financial investment to professionals. There is nothing wrong with having someone else manage your finances if you can't manage them yourself.

It is important that you don't use the excuse of a lack of knowledge as the reason why you don't invest. Acknowledging a lack of knowledge is the greatest step you can take toward investing in yourself. Also, remember the more opportunities that you create for others by creating jobs and helping them become more successful, the more leverage you will have over time. If you open a small business (e.g., a restaurant or a bakery), create a few jobs for some people, and this business eventually pays itself off, you can bring in a company to manage it—and now, through that business, you are able to earn an extra 10% of your income after all expenses are paid and without you having to spend the time to manage it.

In order words, what you have essentially done is created opportunities for those around you and at the same time increased your time. Now you no longer have to physically work for that income. You can repeat that 10% profit endlessly, as long as you are creating value for your customers by providing excellent and affordable food—and, most importantly, creating value for the people who are working for you and their family through work benefits you provide. You are also creating value for your community through the tax support you provide. This is not complicated. All you have to do is create value and view other's interests as your own. Ensure that every endeavor you take and every opportunity you seek will increase not only your value, but also the value of the people around you.

INVESTMENT DURING TIMES
OF FAMINE AND ABUNDANCE

Another misconception about investment is a sense of scarcity. As you might have noted in your life, some people, no matter how fortunate they may be, believe they don't have enough. As a result, they decide that investment is not for them. The reality is, it is important to invest, even if you don't have a lot; otherwise, how else can you develop the habit of investing?

As you have learned in the previous chapters, one of the best ways to detach yourself from a sense of lacking is by being grateful for what you currently have. Otherwise, how else will a single mother working two full-time jobs have the courage to invest in her children without becoming overwhelmed by her sense of lacking? How else could a migrant farmworker have the courage to endure the 80-hour work week doing backbreaking labor in a foreign country where he does not even speak the native language? With eight children and a wife to support in his home country, how could he have the courage to go beyond the feeling of lack and invest in his children and his family?

You may know someone who, despite his or her circumstances, chose to invest in a better tomorrow. You need to appreciate that, no matter where you are in your life, you will experience both the positive and the negative. The question is not which one you have more of in your life; the question is which one you will choose to focus on.

The *7 Checklist Items for Success* encourages you to focus on the positive because what you focus on persists, and such thinking may represent the only flicker of light in the darkness around you. Focusing on the positive (having a positive mental attitude) may be the only candle in the darkness of that single mother's life, or the only glimmer of hope for that farmworker to keep believing and hoping in a better and more successful tomorrow. That hope will shine on not only for himself, but for generations to come. No matter how far behind you are in school, at work, or in your life accomplishments, the checklist to a more successful life encourages you to invest in yourself by reading a little longer, studying a little more, putting in a few more hours, and focusing on yourself a little more. These are the investments we are talking about.

You need to accept and embrace your past while investing in the present for a more abundant future. The sensation of lack, unfortunately, doesn't only originate from your heart. Sometimes the people around you, the people you look up to, or the people who should be encouraging you may feel that you are less than worthy. While I hope that you have never and will never experience this tragedy, the truth remains most people have been through this. The good news is that you can always overcome tragedy. The key to overcoming it is by investing in yourself.

MAKE SURE THAT THOSE WHO INVEST IN YOU NEVER LOSE THEIR INVESTMENT

Always keep the people who have invested in you in focus. If tomorrow you were to go to the bank and withdraw the money you made from investing, only to find out that the bank has burned down with all your life savings, you would probably feel devastated (even if the government promised to refund it). How about the people who have invested in you? Many times, we focus our attention on investing in ourselves and others, but we sometimes fail to give credit to those around us who have invested in us. Think of the parents who worked extremely hard to give their child the opportunity they could only have dreamed of; the teacher who believed in the failing student even when she did not yet believe in herself; the person who was there for a friend through thick and thin; the spouse who believed in his partner even during her lowest moments, and the children who constantly look up in search of a role model. All of these are investments in you, and it is your duty to keep your end of the bargain and commit to your goals. While the person on the receiving end of those commitments should certainly be willing to do anything for the people who invested in him, the only reason they invested in him in the first place was so that *he* could become successful. Their hope is that he never forgets them and always keeps their memory at the forefront of all he does.

Your actions to commit to a more successful life each day are the dividends on their investment. Don't cheat them and don't cheat yourself into giving them anything less than your highest value. There will be a time when you just want to close the blinds, go somewhere no one can ever find you, and just be invisible. This is an option you do not have; people have already invested too much in you. Do your part, follow through with your checklist for a more successful life by writing down your goals, take action by committing the first two hours of your life each day toward their realization, have the courage to remain committed to the realization of your goals no matter what life throws at you, value the resources around you, and keep investing in yourself.

While investing in yourself and those around you is by far the most reliable vehicle to take you to a more successful financial life, you can be certain that the road will have obstacles. You should take courage in the knowledge that others, through integrity and commitment, have successfully traveled that same road to a successful end. All you need to do is remain committed. This is how you ensure that those who invested in you do not lose their investment. This is what giving back is all about.

CHAPTER 6
GIVING BACK

Don't wait until you make it before you give back. Your cup doesn't have to be spilling over before you can start sharing the drink of hope for a more successful future with a thirsty soul in the desert of life. Seek to know what people around you want in life and help them get it. While it can be an uphill battle to become successful, always remember that just like a father wants the life of his children to be better than his own, so is the desire of your Creator. While you are on your quest to a more successful life (and even after realizing your goals), seek to invest in people. The truth is most people want to be successful, but the key is also to want to help others be successful. The problem is most people don't know where to start and are sometimes focused too much on what they do not have (e.g., lack of experience, lack of money, physical limitations). Whatever you focus on will persist, grow, and continue to be the center of your focus and attention. It is counter intuitive to focus on what's lacking when you want to become successful.

GIVE BACK MORE THAN YOU RECEIVE

When you look back on your life, you'll likely realize that the biggest gifts you received toward investing in your future were gifts of encouragement (e.g., from your parents, a teacher, friends, etc.). The checklist for a more successful life encourages you to give more than you have received. How about you start by giving more gifts of encouraging words rather than the generalized slander that is bountiful in the world today? How about saying thank you more? Give more praise and credit to your spouse, child, or coworker who is doing more good than she knows.

How about you start giving the gift of a smile to those around you? A smile to that drive-through fast-food worker can be worth more than any tip you could give them. How about you start complimenting those around you? Compliment them on the success that they have achieved thus far. Compliment them on their goals and their steadfastness and commitment to excellence. Make it a habit of asking others what you can do for them. There is power in serving others genuinely.

If you have ever read the story of Marriott from *The Spirit to Serve Marriott's Way* by J. W. Marriott and Kathy Ann Brown, you will likely conclude the main reason why Marriott went from a few thousand dollars to a multi-billion-dollar company is because of its insatiable desire to serve its customers. I hope you make the decision that so many successful people make and that is to do what works and avoid reinventing the wheel. Always seek to create new paths when a new opportunity comes, but don't stray into thorns in your attempt to do so. Why don't you decide to adopt the winning attitude of Marriott by serving others daily? Serving people with the utmost respect and truly desiring to help is the definition of giving back. What you will undoubtedly realize once you have served others by giving back is that they will unselfishly give back to you. They also want to come back to buy your service whether that service is a clinic, a law-firm, a restaurant, a hotel, or a real estate agency. No matter what your business is or what type of work you do, providing excellent service to people is an all-round win-win situation.

I am sure you are probably reading this book and thinking that such advice will definitely not work in favor of government workers like the teller at your local Department of Motor Vehicles. All the DMV workers have a few things in common. Their workers work very hard, yet they are underappreciated by most of the customers. If you've ever been to a DMV, or especially work at a DMV, you know that the above is not an overstatement. I would argue that the Department of Motor Vehicles, or whatever the equivalent is in your country, is where the greatest need of serving others can be found. Think about it: The job of any government is to serve its people, and the DMV is where everyone in the community goes to have their identification card made, driving license registered, and many other things. The DMV is the place where the local government has a chance to display its spirit to serve its members. Honestly, if every DMV teller showed the true spirit of serving, I am sure, very soon the attitude of the customers would be more positive, and they would have fewer issues coming to the DMV in the first place.

Giving back to others in the form of service is the cure to feeling underappreciated. I hope that when you finish reading this chapter, you will realize that returning more to others, more than you have received, is by far the greatest way to generate more value for your service, your brand, your company, yourself, and for the people around you.

BE EMPATHETIC

Giving back more than you have received does not only pertain to money. One of the most generous things that you can give back to others is your time by encouraging and showing them what it takes to become successful. An important fact to understand about those who have financial success and those who do not is the following: Those who are financially wealthy in our society tend to criticize the non-successful people because they falsely attribute their lack of financial success to a lack of trying or laziness. Whereas the "have nots" tend to attribute financial success to luck, as if they were born with a silver spoon in their mouths or because they are members of the rich club. Like most serious issues in life, the truth sometimes lies inside the gray zone.

Let's try to explain a few misconceptions with the hope that you will understand why, upon reaching a more successful life, your time is one of your two most valuable resources that you can give back to others by teaching the checklist to a more successful life. First, let us address the concern of the first group: those who choose to believe that the "have nots" do not try hard enough, or are not pulling themselves up by their bootstraps. Yet the have nots may not yet realize the truth that they are the captains of their ships and in control of their own destinies. They may not yet know, believe, or accept the self-evident truth that Napoleon Hill spoke of when he said, "Anything the human mind can conceive and believe, it can achieve." If you not only work hard, but also remain committed no matter what to making your goals a reality, they will surely come to fruition, or you will discover goals worthier of your time along the way.

As you can imagine, it is easier to have empathy for people who align with your belief system. But empathy should be extended especially to those who do not share our way of thinking. The idea that as an individual you are in control of your life is a concept inculcated in the wealthy, usually from an early age, reinforced by their environment, and one that they naturally accept as a self-evident truth. Without empathy, how else can wealthy people put themselves in the shoes of those who are deprived of hope and feel helpless in their current situation?

Unlike those who feel that they are in control of their destiny, generally speaking, the have nots in our society have been taught that they will never amount to anything and usually live in communities that reinforce these beliefs. Soon, they, too, will come to accept these lies as their self-evident truth. They've learned these lies from their parents, teachers, and the people around them, but the key concept to understand is that the "haves" believe self-evidently that anything that anyone wants in life can be attained as long as one is willing to work for it. Those who have not, however, even after discovering the truth that they are in control of their destiny, will say they believe anything is possible as long as one is willing to work very hard for it. While the beliefs of these two groups may seem the same, the have nots are still at a disadvantage, at the very least starting with nothing or in dire circumstances that are harder to escape. Nevertheless, it is still possible just like it has been for countless successful people throughout the world. Anything is possible.

It does not matter if you are from a rich or poor family, a black family or white family, a poor country or a rich country, we can all agree that achieving financial success will be difficult, and even more difficult for those who start with less. What those in this first group (the haves) sometimes fail to realize is that the have nots do not believe in themselves or do not have the support of their parents or mentors and lack an environment to reinforce the truth that anything is possible in life.

Those who start with less somehow believe the greatest lie ever told, and the worst part is that they are reinforcing this learned helplessness by believing that there is no way out. They believe that the system is rigged against them, so they might as well accept their lot in life, because—no matter what they do—nothing will change. Jesus was right when he said in Mathew 8:13 that "As you have believed, so shall it be done unto you." The truth is, if these words from Mathew 8:13 and other words of faith, hope, belief, abundance, possibility, and opportunity were to be taught to the have nots every day, it would not be long before that attitude is instilled, and they accepted those ideas as self-evident.

What the first group forgets most of the time is that the opposite is also true. If a person who would otherwise have been born to a wealthy family was born to a needy family, they grow up to be needy. This is not passing the blame; the truth is that the problem is complex. If you were to be exposed to an environment of lack, abuse, belittlement, cheating, murder, and hopelessness, it would not be long before you also accepted that way of life as your truth and acted in a fashion consistent with that environment. This is why it is important to be empathetic of other's misunderstanding of your situation and your passion to change it. This is sad, but it is the truth.

The second group is not blameless, either. Those who believe that they somehow can't succeed because of their situation have a misconception. You have God-given desires that were placed inside you for a reason. Your desire is that thing that stirs up your soul and that makes you want to go on each day. You may not truly know what it is, but you can start by listening to your heart and asking yourself what it is that you were created for. Why you and not somebody else? Why are you lucky enough to be here when so many around you have gone under? *Why?* You need to start by finding your *why* in life. Following these seven checklist items for more success in life will show you the *how*.

GIVING BACK YOUR TIME IS THE FOUNDATION OF TRUST

The above is a tough conversation to have because in both cases, right or wrong, people accept their answer as self-evident and believe it at their core. We need to understand that it is extremely difficult to change our core values. We need to learn to listen to others and understand their stories to create trust. Only when the other person trusts you will they be willing to work with you and accept the possibility that their values may need to be re-examined. To achieve the change they want, they need to start by changing their core belief to that of what Jesus spoke of in Matthew 8:13.

Giving back your time is the foundation of trust; spend the time to listen in order to build rapport. Pay attention and observe what others are doing well. Never miss an opportunity to help. Always remember that examples are the best teachers, so seek to be that example to those around you. Strive to be the reflection of that person whom you wish others could be like. Will you fail at times? Yes. What is important is not how many times you fail at trying to do your best; instead, what matters is that you keep doing your best. If you can take a little time out of the day and devote it to people, the people you help will see that and acknowledge it; you will come to understand the simple fact that YOU matter and that YOUR words can and will have significant impact on other people's lives. It is your responsibility to keep doing your best to make sure that these words are positive and uplifting. You will always get a return on those investments in the end. They are indeed a valuable treasure to you and to those around them.

What about trust? Once you become more successful, you will find it easier to trust others, and you will be excited to help them discover their sources of joy and achievement. Remember, however, that others may not necessarily trust you the same way. They might view you as simply someone lucky who won the jackpot. They may be determined to take or gain any advantage that they can from you. Your trust in people has to be validated.

If you find someone in need of your mentorship whom you decide to help with your time, do so to the best of your ability just like you know someone would do for you under the same circumstances. If you discover that that person does not sincerely want to succeed, however, or to excel, commit, or follow through with goals, you need to stop investing your time.

Remember, your time is your greatest resource. For example, if you have someone whom you mentor for one hour each month, you can start by asking her to read the *7 Checklist Items for Success* or any other book you believe will help. You can also tell her to prepare 25 goals for her next visit. If, for some reason during the next month, that person did not complete this assignment, this should be your sign that this person is not determined at this time to achieve a more successful life. Discontinue the mentorship.

This does not mean that person will not be willing, one day, to commit to what it takes to achieve success. It only means he is not ready at this time. Whenever he is ready, he will already have a book to start with. The same advice applies to you. If you are working with a coach or a mentor, it is your obligation to do your best and do your part. Remember, you can only give back after you have earned something. You cannot expect someone you are mentoring to commit to a more successful life if you are not committed to doing the same. Always remember that your actions are stronger than your words. Be the leader who your people know will never ask them to do something that you wouldn't do yourself. The foundation of trust is built by action, not by talking the talk.

THE PHILOSOPHY OF LIVING A MORE SUCCESSFUL LIFE

Once you are able to detach yourself from a sense of lack, you will be able to tap into your true potential in life, which is the ability to experience that sense of freedom and limitlessness that comes from being successful. A sense of abundance will help you understand that no matter what the current level of success in your life is, you have something to give back, and you matter as a human being. No matter how bad your situation is, you have yourself and your time to create more value for yourself and those around you. A sense of abundance will also create riches as limitless as those of the wealthiest people on earth. By now it's obvious to you that you can use your twenty-four hours for productive and constructive endeavors that make life a little better for those around you—just like you can waste that time in unproductive behaviors of gossip, drunkenness, and laziness.

My hope is that you will claim your birthright as the child of the Almighty God who made you this promise in Haggai 2:8, "The silver is mine and the gold is mine." My hope is that you will decide to believe what countless other successful people have believed throughout the years: Resources are limitless, and all around us! With such a faith in abundance, when you give back to others, you will not feel that you are depleting your resources. Instead, you will feel blessed by the opportunity of knowing at your core that you are giving back the gift of courage and opportunity.

All you have to do is believe in your desires and your goals by knowing the simple fact that simply having these desires and goals is proof enough that they can become your reality. As Jesus told his followers in Mathew 8:13, "Go! Let it be done just as you believed it would." Yet so many among us have chosen not to believe this truth, and instead of using this principle to our advantage to think of abundance and success, we focus on our lack and failures. It is important you understand that just like the thoughts of your mind have power, the words from your mouth also have power.

Moving forward, you need to understand that and decide what the gift of your words to others will be. Will they be words of lacking, defeat, discouragement, self-doubt, and regret? Or will they be words of abundance, success, blessing, encouragement, confidence, and hope? The choice is yours—and, honestly, your brain will not care which one you choose. As your dedicated servant, your wishes are its command. What are the commands you want to execute in this world? Based on the fact that you have read this far, I pray it will be more hope, more gratitude, more positive mental attitudes, and the commitment to create a more successful life not just for yourself, but also for others. After all, in the big scheme of things, it does not matter how little or how much you have received; what matters is how much hope and opportunity for a more successful life you have given to others. Seek always to give more than you have received, to love more than you have been loved, and create and entrust more opportunities to others than have been entrusted to you.

GIVE WITH OPEN HANDS

You have often heard people say, "What one hand gives, the other hand doesn't have to know." Such advice reminds us that the purpose of giving is not for our self-gratification or to brag to the world. Giving for such narrow purposes is obviously wrong. Giving back should be done with the sole purpose of creating value in the life of the person in front of you. When it comes to giving back, either to the people around us or to our community, remember that life is not a fight. You cannot give with a fist as if you are forcing others to do what you want. Instead, giving back should be done solely with the intent of helping people reach their full potential by developing their core competencies and values.

When giving, both your hands and your heart have to be open. Your heart has to be open to see all human beings for who they are (the image of the Almighty God), then love and respect them as such. Your hands must be open to embracing those in need and giving others the opportunities you wish you had been given earlier. Give back by believing in those around you to inspire hope and giving them the confidence that they are valuable. Help them discover that their true treasure lies within them.

At first, it might be difficult for you and your mentee to forgo the fears of being exploited. No matter how absurd such a thought may seem to you, those in need are often being taken advantage of by the very people who pretend to help them—even those in charge of protecting them. Even those in need sometimes take advantage of the people who are trying to help them. As you will soon realize, once trust is established, giving back opportunities is the surest way to improve the lives of the people around you; all you have to do is to ask someone about their dreams and aspirations, then expose them to the opportunities for realizing those dreams.

Will this be easy? The answer is no. But life is not easy. Life is about improving the circumstances of people around you. When you become more successful, more people around you will have their own ideas of how they want you to help them. Unfortunately, many times they ask for cash, cash, and more cash. Don't blame them. Remember, they still have the mindset that they need money to be successful. They have not yet realized that money is just a by-product of a more successful life. They don't know that by receiving the knowledge to create a more valuable life, you have given them something that is more valuable than money.

In fact, once they become more successful, they will realize that money is overrated, and they will realize what you have given them is actually a life treasure: the treasure of being more successful. When I was fifteen, I met an engineer named Roger through a network marketing business. He was the most successful man that I knew in my circle at that time. Roger soon became someone I looked up to. I recall one day Roger asked me what my goals in life were. I was taken aback by the question; I did not know how to answer. He rephrased the question and asked what I wanted to accomplish in my life. I told him that I was not sure and that I didn't have a clear direction of where I wanted to go in life. I told him that I didn't have the example of a role model and father figure to follow after my dad left for the United States in 1984. I have never forgotten the answer that Roger gave that day. He told me that in life there will always be plenty of opportunities to find excuses, and that my statement of not having a functional family was an excuse that anyone could use in their own family.

He then told me what I have since considered to be my greatest treasure in life. He told me that, through books, I could find all the role models I ever wanted, from the dead to the living. He also told me that through books, I could find the advice from the father figure I had been yearning for. Roger was sincere, his words were kind, and he was patient with me. Somehow, I believed his words and have held onto them over the years. I have since lost contact with Roger, but I cannot wait for the day when I meet him again and look him in the eyes to say thank you. Thank you for giving me the greatest gift in life. Roger's gift to me was the gift of hope.

He told me where my ultimate treasure could eventually be found. I was reassured knowing that my treasure could be found in books, even though I did not know which book. The search has been an interesting one. One that has taken me from a confused and timid fifteen-year-old who viewed himself as impoverished to a physician and Naval Officer in the greatest navy in the world. This is indeed the power of giving back. This book is the result of Roger's giving back to me; now it is yours. I am giving it to you with open hands. It is now your responsibility to use this gift not only for a more successful life for yourself, but also for the world. I hope and pray that your gift back to the world will be even more valuable.

WORDS FROM YOUR MOUTH ARE WORTH MORE THAN GOLD

Psalm 119:72 says of the Almighty God, "The law from your mouth is more precious to me than thousands of pieces of silver and gold." Our words are so powerful. They help us not only change our lives, but also to change the lives of those around us. Think of the case of a Navy Senior Chief, for example. I always find it perplexing to meet a Senior Chief who retires from the Navy and, after 10 years of retirement, is now obese and physically out of shape to a point that his sailors barely recognize him. You may ask yourself, "What happened? Why does that Senior Chief, who was once considered a model of excellence, fail to maintain for himself the same level of excellence he had inculcated to his younger sailors and Junior Officers for so many years?" The answer to this question is the power of commitment. Commitment is doing the things you said that you would do the moment you said them and the moments directly after you said them. It doesn't matter if that moment is one hour after, one day after, or the moment before you die, commitment is simply doing the things that you said you would do. Commitment is waking up at 4 a.m. no matter what, every single day of your life to work toward the realization of your goals.

What happens to the Senior Chief in our example is that he stops committing to the level of excellence he taught his younger sailors. Why has he stopped being committed to the excellence that he valued so dearly for many years? It's a question that we all can ask ourselves. Why do you stop dreaming the dreams you had when you were little? Why do you stop being fearless, like you used to be when you were in your teenage years? Why do you stop smiling like you used to when you were a baby? Why?

I believe the answer to these questions is because of the people we choose to associate with in life. It is likely that when you are around happy and motivated people, you will feel the same as them: happy and motivated. The challenge is once we have stopped being happy and motivated, how do we become happy and motivated again? When the happy bunch avoids the unhappy friend, this is not because they don't love this friend anymore. It happens because that friend stopped being who he was created to be. The key to happiness, the treasure key, is to find your "it" factor. The key to having energy and enjoying every moment of your life is finding your core values and making the decision to remain committed to those values. Promise yourself that you will remain committed until your last breath. Keep giving back opportunities to others so that they may also find their passion. Give with open hands. May the words of your mouth exude joy, energy, and enthusiasm as the testament of them is worth more than gold for the treasure hunter who seeks them.

A MORE SUCCESSFUL LIFE IS ABOUT GIVING BACK

By now, you have realized that giving back is about raising people up. It is about being on the side of people when they feel alone in this world. It is about helping the elderly and encouraging the young. Giving back is about knowing that you are not alone in your journey to a more successful life and that you are responsible for leaving clues of your success on the path of life for those who come behind you to follow. Giving back is about you being the light to those who look up to you and leaving footsteps on the path to a more successful life. Giving back should transcend partisanship, race, or social status and focus only on other's desires, dreams, and aspirations for success.

It is easy to live a life of waiting to see how much others can give you, but choosing to live a life where your motto is to ask others what you can do for them will warrant a far more satisfying intrinsic return. While it is always a good thing to say thank you and show appreciation, your goals should be to go out there and serve others and to be the one who praises, compliments, and blesses others the most. Once you decide to invest your time in helping others, you will find more effective ways to reach people, whether through social media or a book.

The ultimate measure of a more successful life (if such a thing were to exist) wouldn't be judged by your personal achievement, but instead how many people you helped along the way. Others may look at your life and see the house you have, your net worth, or notable things you did, but in the end, your true yardstick should always be the positive value you have created in the lives of those around you and beyond. Everything is intrinsic and helping others usher in that feeling like nothing else.

You should not care about keeping score but should strive to always give back whenever and wherever you see the need. You have to give back, whether that is as simple as explaining these seven checklist items to a high school student or as difficult as giving back hope to an elderly woman desiring to leave her mark behind in the sand of life. You should strive to give back the opportunity for a more successful life to the single mother who doesn't have the time or the energy to go on. You should strive to give back the hope to the young man or woman who is uncertain about the future. You should strive to give back encouragement by showing the path to a more successful life to the men and women who are not proud of their past, unsatisfied with their present, and uncertain about their future.

WHY GIVE BACK?

This book was not intended to explain the why of things. It was merely intended to state what works as a guide, so you could follow the points as a checklist and be successful. But since every rule has an exception and due to the counterintuitive aspect of giving back when the idea of a more successful life seems to imply that we should self-ishly acquire more value, I will try to explain why giving is important.

First, let's clear up some confusion. I have always thought it was strange that the same God who declared in Haggai 2:8, "The silver is mine and the gold is mine" would ask His people in Deuteronomy 14:22 to "Be sure to set aside a tenth of all that your field produce each year" to give to his sanctuary. For a long time, these two verses never made sense to me. I felt somehow that they were placed in the Bible to trick to me. Later, I wanted to believe that God put Deuter-onomy 14:22 in the Bible so that His sanctuary could provide me with the necessary funds to solve my problems. I could never amass enough courage to share this last idea with my preacher for fear of being excommunicated.

Needless to say, my wishes did not come true and my confu-sion deepened. Then, during a sermon, a preacher explained that giving back 10% of what we earn yearly is not for God's own sake; he surely doesn't need it. The preacher explained that God asks us to give him 10% of what we make for our own sake. He asks 10% from us as a way to free us of the false beliefs of lacking, that we don't have enough, and that only the rich should give. It may sound strange, but somehow when we give, it creates a sense of abundance within us. Maybe that is the sense of abundance God wants us to feel as children of the Almighty King and not as children of the Earth striving to gain riches. Giving imparts in the you, the donor, a sense of prosperity since you cannot give what you do not have.

If you don't trust this, try to give a check to your bank when you don't have the funds to clear it and you will soon understand. On a more serious note, you would likely agree that you can only give appreciation for what you appreciate, just like you can only give love to what you love. Giving back creates a sense of accomplishment within you and a sense that you are worth something because you have something to give. Giving back will empower you with the knowledge that you are making a difference. The confidence that you are making a difference will then empower you to know that you *can* make a difference. Knowing that you can make a difference empowers you to resolve within yourself that if you can, then you **must** make a difference.

Take, for example the missionary groups who, over the years, decided to conduct routine mission trips to help people in Mole Saint Nicholas, an isolated city located in the northwestern part of Haiti. These groups assist the needy and bring hope to this community. If you were one of the members who donated to that church group, you cannot feel but proud of yourself of what this group has done. This group has made a difference. The same is true for you each time you contribute your resources to a volunteer or donate to a non-profit organization that is doing serious work to improve the world and creating more successful lives for people.

You will get to a point in your life where you will realize that one of the greatest truths is that you can gain more by giving and you can give more than you have received. Why does this truth work this way? I don't know, and honestly don't think it is important. This is simply one of those times in life where I just press the "I believe" button and carry on. Just like you feel safer when you know that others around are keeping an eye on you, those around you also feel safer to know that you are keeping an eye on them.

In fact, when you feel that you have nothing to give, that's the perfect time to go out of your comfort zone and give back to others. If you think this is not possible, think again. Think of the story of Viktor Frankl in *Man's Search for Meaning*. It is possible that even in your deepest despair and sorrow you can give back to those around you. When you do, you'll transcend from "you, the individual" to "you, as a member of the collective."

In addition to finding a moment at the end of each day to reflect on what you are grateful for, I will add that during that time, you should also reflect each evening on what you have given back or what good you did that day. This will not be overwhelming. It will only remind you to be more conscious of the need around you and the difference you are making in people's lives. It is my goal that the *7 Checklist Items for Success* will one day help you consider an alternative to living a life so few have ever dared to consider.

I hope that you realize you were created not just for the mere enjoyment of life, but instead to enjoy creating a lifelong difference in people's lives. Giving back can help you find your purpose in life and, as a result, create a legacy for yourself every day. Moving onto the next chapter, I hope to help convince you that if given a choice you will join me to choose that a legacy should not be created at the end one's life but is only revealed at the end of one's life.

CHAPTER 7
LEGACY:
CREATE A LEGACY OF SERVICE TO OTHERS

May your legacy be one of giving back and making a difference in the lives of people around you. Moving forward, you can lay the path to your legacy by applying the acts of kindness you have received along the way to your current situation. Move forward seek to perform more acts of kindness to others and give more in terms of the time you spend with them, the smiles you bestow on them, and the words of encouragement you speak unto them. Each one of us on this Earth is too precious and too rare to leave this world without making a positive impact in the life of those around us and the lives of those who will come after us.

In the previous chapter, you learned about giving back. You probably now have the answer to the question that many people ask, which is: How much should they give? You may also ask when to start giving. Sometimes, you may feel that you do not have enough; therefore, you cannot give. All these are good concerns and there are no right or wrong answers.

One of the first self-help books that I read as a teenager was written by the late Zig Ziglar and was titled *See You at the Top*. Zig Ziglar was correct when he said, "Where you start is not nearly as important as where you finish," and that you should never let the challenges of your past prevent you from reaching a more successful life. It is important to remember that we started in this world with nothing. We took our first breath and that was our first act in this world, and we will return that gift as we depart it as well.

No matter how unsatisfying the above statement may seem, you need to understand that the true meaning of your existence is governed by what you do during the time that elapses between these two breaths. Your biggest gift as a human being is the way you choose to deal with any situation in life and the fact that you have control over your circumstances. You can either react with positive or negative behavior. If you choose to view life positively, you need to take advantage of all the moments afforded to you between these two breaths—not just for the sake of living, but for the sake of making a difference in this world because you have been in it and the difference you make in your life is your legacy.

Your legacy does not start after you depart this world, but it should be the fabric of your existence, bridging your lowest point to your current life and your current life bridging you to a more successful future. From this point on in your life, you should keep looking forward to the potential of what the future will be in terms of the difference you want to make. This is the legacy you want to leave behind.

Moving forward, you can lay the path to your legacy by focusing on giving back the acts of kindness you have received along the way. You should strive to be kind to others in terms of the time you spend with them, the smile you bestow on them, and the words of encouragement you speak to them. Each one of us on this earth is too precious and too rare to leave this world in-between these two breathes without making a positive impact.

What will your impact be? It is up to you. You just have to listen to the voice inside of you asking you the question, "What is the purpose of your life?" Honestly, it is the same voice that will give you the answer. Once you know the answer to that question, all you have to do is to write your goals down, plan on how to make your goals become a reality, and then take action daily toward the realization of these goals. The rest will be history, a history engraved with the footprint of your legacy, that is.

AIM TO CREATE A LEGACY OF HOPE

Leaving behind a legacy usually has its roots in an attitude of gratitude. When you think about it, people who feel they have more to be grateful for are usually those who feel they have more to give. As a result, they leave a legacy behind as a clue to their success. If you compare and contrast your current moment with the lowest moment of your life, you are likely to find reasons to be grateful for your current situation. The fallacy we face sometimes is that false sense that our life has to be perfect and must remain perfect before we can bring change, make a difference, and leave a legacy behind.

But the point in life is not to be perfect, because you already have perfection within. It would be an insane feat to go searching all around the world for the treasure that you already possess, but that is exactly what most of us do in our life. No one can create a legacy by chasing his tail, and if you are to leave a legacy behind, the first thing you need to do is claim your throne of the more perfect life kingdom within you as the child of the Almighty God, created in His image. You are the being in control of creating a more perfect and more successful life daily, through your actions.

Your legacy starts when you begin to be the best you can be in everything that you do through relentless, continual improvement. Aim to be the best version of yourself by being kinder to others and a beacon of hope for them to see. Live each day with the goal of leading a life consistent with the legacy you want to leave behind. While such a legacy may not be perfect, the point is that through your daily actions, you should aim at making it more perfect with each passing day.

The reason why many of us fail to strive for a more perfect life is, unfortunately, because we fail to realize we already have that perfection within. Your job is to reclaim your perfection, to strive to make it a little better every day, and to go a little further each new day. You need to realize that the limitation of your own thinking is the very thing that limits the kind of legacy that you can leave behind. Once you realize your goals, let that be the proof for your life that abundance and success are all around you and the purpose of your journey in life is to follow that bliss and aim to make whatever gives you that bliss more perfect each day. In return, you understand that you've never worked a day in your life because you enjoy it.

A LEGACY AND A WAY OF LIFE

May your legacy be a legacy of giving opportunities to others and a legacy of light to those who have lost their purpose, a legacy of teaching to those who seek a more successful life. Through your legacy of giving, you will discover that the attainment of a more successful life is possible. May your legacy of giving stimulate those around you to embrace their passion, excel in it, and use it to make life better.

It is possible that your legacy may be bigger than what you can even conceive, so dream big. Do not let your setbacks of the past or the challenges of the present restrict your mind's eye from conceiving the vision of the possibilities that the future can bring. Trust and believe in the impossible. You may think that it's impossible to create a legacy when you have not even achieved the more successful life you are pursuing. It is important to remember, however, that the line separating the impossible and the possible is thinner than you know. And more often than not, all it takes to turn what others have told you was impossible is just you daring to believe and commit yourself to act toward the realization of whatever it is you want to achieve. Miracles are possible only to the believers. Living your life the way you want to be remembered should be the compass guiding you through the sea of self-doubt and feelings of inadequacy that we sometimes erroneously believe is our destiny.

You can bring yourself to believe that you can achieve whatever it is that you desire and are passionate about instead of doubting yourself or finding excuses for not. It is not surprising that most people can realize a life of more success. What is surprising is that so many people believe they cannot reach a more successful life when in fact all they have to do is to emulate the life of successful people around them. A life of more success is possible, and indeed it is your destiny and purpose to live such a life.

Ideas of great success have come to you many times in the past and will come to you many more times in the future. What is important is that you take action and act on those ideas immediately and make sure you write them down and commit to take daily action until you accomplish them. You will be surprised to see that most of the goals you thought were impossible will be your reality 5 to 10 years down the road.

Just like a guided missile can reach any target it is programmed to locate, you can also accomplish anything that you desire if you create and apply goals. What you may not realize is that even the guided missile needs to make constant readjustments before hits its target. The same concept applies to you. Even though your creator, the Almighty God, created you for a purpose or target in life, you need to create goals and take action to guide you to your destination and the accomplishment of your desires. The difference between you and that guided missile is that your Heavenly father created you with free will; you have the free will to doubt yourself, procrastinate, and not commit to following through with His plans. The guided missile does not have a free will; once it is engaged, it remains committed.

How about you? Now that you are engaged with the *7 Checklist Items for Success*, can you remain committed? You're almost halfway through the last chapter so hopefully that answer is a resounding *yes!* In a sense, you can think of your free will as what differentiates you from a machine or another species. Your free will was given to you as a gift allowing you to oversee your life, channel your potential to whatever it is that you want, and operate on manual function instead of an automatic one. Use that gift to see the needs around you, then apply yourself to meet those needs to build a legacy that will also help others to reach their full potential.

The fact that you cannot yet see that destination, or the realization of your goal, does not mean that the goal is impossible; it only means that your human eyes are not yet in range. You have to find and maintain the faith that your Heavenly Father made you according to His perfection and made no mistakes. In fact, if you keep the faith and remain consistent, it is impossible that you will not reach your goals. The key to the realization of any goal and the key to leaving the legacy that you want is never to give up, but instead move through life with confidence and always seek to give back.

HUMAN LIMITATION AND A LEGACY THAT SHOWS WILL IS LIMITLESS

As a living being, you are limited by time. Unfortunately, one day you will depart this earth. The good news is that your legacy can be limitless. The best way to ensure that your legacy will pass the test of time is to live a life consistent with the value of integrity as you remain 100% committed to the realization of your goals. The key to leaving a legacy that will pass the test of time is to also live a life where you never forget that the world is bigger than you. People do not revolve around you, but you should make sure your life revolves around others. Your legacy should always be focused on leaving the door of opportunity open behind you, no matter how hard you had to work to open it for yourself.

The best way to leave a legacy is to realize that your success in life does not diminish when more people become more successful, but instead you are more successful with them. Creating a legacy is not focusing on what the critics say about you, but instead staying focused on creating opportunities to increase the value of resources around you. It is always remaining focused on achieving the ultimate goal of your passion while being flexible and adapting to new situations along the way.

As you continue to follow your passion, your bliss, or your flow, whatever the name you want to call it, you will realize that there is no need to dedicate any special time to creating a legacy because your legacy is the difference that you are making through following your passion. In other words, your legacy is a product of realizing your fullest potential in life. You will also come to see at some point that if there ever were an enemy to realizing a more successful life, that enemy is self-doubt. Self-doubt about whether you will ever be successful, whether you will ever graduate, whether you will ever be able to find a partner. The list goes on and on. Self-doubt is always the wrong answer. The key is to find out whatever it is that you were created for. Mastering it will be a joy and you will find that even taking a lunch break from it is painful. It will keep you up at night, and you'll still be excited about it.

While the answers to all the above questions are important, your goal is to find the passion that will serve as the conduit to help you express your internal world to the outside one. You will come across some people in this world (you might even be one them) who have found their passion in life. They may explain that when performing or doing that passion they feel like a god or goddess. It transports them to a new world in the moment. Surprisingly, I find myself asking why I don't read about these people or see them on TV. It is sad to say, but too often self-doubt is what prevents people from breaking the glass ceiling of whatever their barrier is.

If self-doubt is what prevents you from achieving your full potential, why don't you cut it off? Many of the tentacles of self-doubt may be wrapped around you. They can be in the forms of envy, lies, greed, and many others. You would be better off to cut them all off if you want to reach the fullest potential of your passion, make a difference, or create a legacy.

A LEGACY OF ENCOURAGEMENT

There are a lot of people out there who want to hear that anything is possible in life—no matter where people come from—as long as they are willing to commit to the realization of their goals toward a more successful life. The need for encouragement exists. You can start such a legacy today; it does not have to wait until you have it in abundance.

If you see someone who's in need of food, especially women and children, you would not wait until you have plenty to feed them because you know they will get weak and eventually die before you could amass such food. The same is true when you are not helping those around you to believe in themselves. Most of those people you interact with don't see the potential you see in them. During your journey to a more prosperous life, you will meet a great number of individuals who may have the desire for a more successful life or even have a passion in life that they would like to pursue, but for some reason are afraid to take the steps toward achieving their goals.

As I said earlier, those who are not committed to their dreams sometimes need some words of encouragement from those around them. Why are you afraid to reach out? They need to know that it is okay to fail to accomplish their daily goals and that in fact most successful people routinely overestimate the daily goals and underestimate the long-term goals. Or altogether just fail to realize their goals in general sometimes. They need the encouragement of knowing if, in the event they were to fail to achieve a specific goal, that at the very least they now know what it's like to have tried something great. It is very easy for self-doubt and fear to paralyze an individual from taking action by fearing others will ridicule them.

The truth is, there will be setbacks that will prevent you from achieving your goal. Whatever those setbacks might be, you will still be ahead of the game because you have gained the advantages of starting. Instead of letting the fear of failure paralyze you, focus on being the leader whose legacy is hope, a smile, and encouragement to people; be the one whispering to them in a calm voice to remain committed, not to give up, and that everything will be okay.

May your voice of encouragement be stronger and louder than their own voices of fear and self-doubt. Through your actions and your behavior, you will have the opportunity to plant hope in the heart of the hopeless. Get them to believe that anything they can conceive in their mind and believe, they can achieve, just like Napoleon Hill noted. Encourage them to believe and understand that life is not limited in abundance and that our abundance is only limited by our self-doubt and fear.

CREATE A LEGACY OF OPPORTUNITIES FOR OTHERS

This book has instructed you to start with five goals because, by the time you have realized your top five goals in life, you will already be making a significant difference in the lives of those around you— and as a result, you will be creating a legacy. Once you have realized those five goals, you will need to be ready to have another goal and that is to continuously keep creating value and making a difference in the life of those around you. Hopefully, in your lifetime, you will see the result of creating your legacy.

In the rare event where you were not to get the recognition that is rightly yours, you should not let that stop you from making a difference in the lives of others. If you really think about it, what difference does it make if the person whom you have helped to realize a more successful life has failed to thank you or show you the gratitude that you deserve? You need to be able to do the same again if the opportunity were to present itself.

Be aware of the danger of pride, because pride is what will cause you to keep looking behind at how much you have accomplished from where you have been, when all that matters is how much more you can do where you are going. This is not to say that your past is not important—it is your past that has brought you to this point—but in terms of making that difference in the future that this book talks about, the important part is the action that you take in the present.

When it comes to helping others to reach their full potential, you need to denude your pride. Creating value in others is not about your pride; it's about making the people around you proud and to always give credit where credit is due. The hope is that you will always be seeking to leave a perfect legacy behind through improvements that you will make on the road to a more successful life.

Where people cannot see the doors of opportunity in front of them, your legacy should be to point and lead them to reach their full potential toward a more successful life. Where those doors do not exist, you should create them. Who knows, maybe at the end of your life when your eulogy is being read, your passion to create a legacy of opportunities for others will fuel an empty fellow human being to go out and create an even a more successful life.

LEGACY, THE ARBITER OF THE GAME OF SUCCESS

Live a life of significance that matters to people and always seek to leave a legacy of caring for others. As you learned earlier, people usually do amazing things for reasons greater than themselves. For example, it's not surprising to see some of the greatest scientists of our time find great pleasure in seeking to solve problems affecting the entire world, not just their personal problems. You will see some of the best physicians take great pleasure in seeking to solve the problem of illnesses affecting others, not just their sickness. On the other hand, it is not surprising to find some of the most selfish people are usually least happy in what they do.

The key to creating a legacy is to help as many people as you can live a more successful life. The sense that you are doing something greater than yourself and for people beyond yourself and your immediate family will probably give your life the greatest sense of purpose. That great sense of purpose is what will allow you to happily go the extra mile. That greater sense of purpose will give you the energy and motivation to wake up long before those around you and to stay more engaged than those around you.

Always seek to answer your *why* questions with answers that create more value in the lives of others. You have probably heard real estate agents talk about a great location and making improvements to create more property value. Apply the same principle in your quest to make a difference and create a legacy. The location is always perfect; it has already been chosen for you. The Creator knows what the best place for you is; it is our planet, Earth. This location was chosen for you by the Greatest Architect, the Almighty God. All you have to focus on is improving and creating more value to the inhabitants of this great location.

Make it your duty and your responsibility in life to create the most beautiful legacy you can think of, desire, or be passionate about. Help others in their enjoyment of life. It is unlikely that this is too difficult of a task for you.

After all, you were created by the hand of the Almighty. He has breathed life into you. He has chosen you among trillions of others; you are special. He called you his greatest possession. He knows every hair on your head. If you still doubt yourself, look in the book of Jeremiah 1:5. Or ask your religious leader. He or she will provide you with plenty more examples, such as Genesis 1:27, Genesis 2:7, Psalm 139:13-16, Matthew 10:30, or Philippians 4:13. The Bible is full of these examples of your true value; they were meant and written for you to know and embrace them.

Your story is even better than Prince Akeem's in "Coming to America." With such a legacy, it only stands to reason that you can indeed create the most beautiful legacy you can think of, desire, and be passionate about. It is crucial that you stop believing in the lies of self-doubt and pessimism and start allowing the legacy of your true origin to be the guide and arbiter of your legacy.

PAY IT FORWARD

No matter where you are currently in your life, it is likely that someone made many sacrifices to help you get here. Maybe grandparents or parents left the comfort of their environment to start an unknown journey to a foreign country in search of a new life, as did my father. Regardless of who made the journey for you, some sacrifices had to be made for you to be where you are now reading this book.

No matter how much you want to believe it is all through your own effort that you have succeeded thus far, deep inside you know there were a lot of invisible hands behind your success: that teacher who believed in you, or that foster parent who gave you a shot at the opportunity you never could have dreamed of.

Now it's you who should return the favor. Will you be one of those people in life who, no matter how much they have achieved, still feel that they do not have enough? Will you keep postponing giving back to society? Will you be that person who says there is too much poverty, abuse, corruption, inequalities, and hopelessness in the world and decides to take action? The choice is yours.

You can start by sharing some words of encouragement with those around you. Make them feel like they are the most important people in the world. Care for them, take the time to ask them about their personal story, ask them how their children are doing, ask them what their inspirations are, and, most importantly, ask them how you can help them. You may be surprised at how much of a difference your caring and your words of encouragement may have on that person who may be going through some marital difficulties, have a sick child, or difficulty managing his or her finances. Just make it your duty to do and stand for what is right with integrity and decency.

May your legacy always push you to remain passionate and enthusiastic about whatever it is that you do to the best of your ability. May your legacy always be one that praises and encourages other people to reach their full potential. May your legacy be one where you always stay true to yourself, understanding that you will not be able to change everything. May your legacy always be one that does not let itself be blinded by past success, but instead seek to leave a legacy of diligent work in the present just as you are focusing on the future.

You can be certain that at times life will be a challenge and discouragement may set in; in these moments of despair, may your legacy be one of gratitude for what you have. Despite all the critics and the problems that you may face, may your legacy be one where you choose to rise above these challenges by learning to see value in each person and help humankind to be more valuable.

How will your legacy be measured? How true legacy is measured does not have anything to do with how much wealth you have or have accumulated, how much wealth that you will accumulate, or the amount of your charitable contributions. Instead, a true legacy is measured by the number of people you help and the value you create in their life. When it comes to creating a legacy, it is your duty as a human to leave this planet better than you have found it. The *7 Checklist Items for Success* was written for you.

May a life of success and a legacy of creating value and hope in others be yours forever.

Thank you,

Dr. Jean G. Mathurin

SUMMARY

Long-term goals and perseverance in taking action for at least 2 hours each morning toward your realization. Review your goals every morning. Write goals for the next day each night.

CONCLUSION

This book has shown you seven ways to challenge yourself to create a more successful life. But why challenge yourself at all? You don't have to look further than how skeletal muscles get stronger, how a lobster grows, or how a diamond is created to find the answer. When you go to the gym, the more you challenge your musculoskeletal muscles by using them against resistance, the stronger and bigger they get. Because of the restrictive challenge posed by its shell, a lobster is only able to grow by shedding its shell. A diamond is only able to form due to intense pressure and temperature. The seven items on the checklist to a more successful life will also push you to the limit. You will find many reasons or excuses not to use these seven checklist items daily, but if you really want to have a more successful life, I dare you to apply them!

My first challenge in life started as my first memory—I could not eat eggs because I could not tolerate the smell. I have learned to go out of my comfort zone, and, over time, I even started to very slowly appreciate eggs. Now I eat them routinely. After you have consistently followed the 7 *Checklist Items for Success* for 5-10 years, you will have one thing in common with most successful people: you will realize that you did not dream big enough after accomplishing all your goals. At the end of this time, you might also realize that even the dreams that you did not accomplish are ok to live without.

For example, you may recall at the beginning that my desire to become a physician was so I could receive turkeys as remuneration for my medical services. Sadly, I have never received such a gift. I figure this will likely never happen; I am ok with that. What I have received in return goes beyond my wildest dream. I have met many very grateful patients, and I feel blessed for the honor to treat and care for some of the most resilient and finest people I have ever known. Working with these people has in return given me the inspiration to follow my deepest desire to help people become successful in life. May these seven checklist items help you achieve your highest heart's desires and, as a result, afford you the opportunity to make a difference in the lives of the people around you.

In this book, few mentions were made of money. Money alone will not furnish a more successful life. While it is true that everybody needs a job, money should never be the sole purpose of your job. You probably have seen an employee at a restaurant who is beaming with joy for the job and a high-profile person who seems to hate everything about the job. Do you ever wonder what the difference is between the two?

The key is to have a job where you feel happy and where you feel you are making a difference. Whether this is working for NASA to push the limit of mankind or working in a corrupt government to bring more transparency and to improve life for the oppressed. The key is to always know the *why* for doing what you do. Make the why your energy source. In our journey on the road of life, most of us spend our lives pursuing money like a blind person. The sad thing is that the treasure we have been looking for has been all around us on the same road all along. That treasure is the expression of your utmost desire and passion; the way all of us can express our truth, our passion, and make a difference. The guide you have been waiting for can be found within the seven items of the checklist for a more successful life presented in this book.

What do you have to do next? All you need to do is simply start now; you can start by writing specific and clear goals about what your desires and passion are. Take daily actions toward the achievements that you want to realize, have the courage to remain committed, always value resources, invest in yourself and those around you, always seek to give back more than you have received, and create a legacy by making a difference. The next thing you know, people's lives will be better because of you.

This book was written as a guide for those of you who feel that there is something more to life than just enjoyment; it is a book for those of you who want to make a difference. It is not a book for everyone. It was written for those of you who know the *why* of your existence. You know your core beliefs, the reason *why* you believe you are here on this earth. You need to start by finding your *why* in this life, and then following the seven items for a more successful life will show you the *how*. You have probably noticed this book was not intended to be a book to read just once, but instead it was intended to be a book to go back to again and again. The 7 *Checklist Items* and its advice should be incorporated into your life every day.

I would like to end this book with a poem by Henry Wadsworth Longfellow. It is one my favorite poems because it shows us the purpose of life is to transcend our challenges. It also shows our obligation to make life a little better for those who will come after us. It will give you a glimpse of what achieving a more successful life can represent for those who come after you. I wish you the very best this world has to offer.

A PSALM OF LIFE

BY HENRY WADSWORTH LONGFELLOW

What The Heart Of The Young Man Said To The Psalmist.

Tell me not, in mournful numbers,
    Life is but an empty dream!
For the soul is dead that slumbers,
    And things are not what they seem.

Life is real! Life is earnest!
    And the grave is not its goal;
Dust thou art, to dust returnest,
    Was not spoken of the soul.

Not enjoyment, and not sorrow,
    Is our destined end or way;
But to act, that each to-morrow
    Find us farther than to-day.

Art is long, and Time is fleeting,
    And our hearts, though stout and brave,
Still, like muffled drums, are beating
    Funeral marches to the grave.

In the world's broad field of battle,
    In the bivouac of Life,
Be not like dumb, driven cattle!
    Be a hero in the strife!

Trust no Future, howe'er pleasant!
  Let the dead Past bury its dead!
Act,— act in the living Present!
  Heart within, and God o'erhead!

Lives of great men all remind us
  We can make our lives sublime,
And, departing, leave behind us
  Footprints on the sands of time;

Footprints, that perhaps another,
  Sailing o'er life's solemn main,
A forlorn and shipwrecked brother,
  Seeing, shall take heart again.

Let us, then, be up and doing,
  With a heart for any fate;
Still achieving, still pursuing,
  Learn to labor and to wait.

17091633R00084

Made in the USA
Middletown, DE
04 December 2018